THE SHEPHERD OF ISRAEL
AND
HIS SCATTERED FLOCK

THE SHEPHERD OF ISRAEL

AND

HIS SCATTERED FLOCK

A Solution of the Enigma of Jewish History

BY

DAVID BARON

Editor of *The Scattered Nation*

AUTHOR OF "THE ANCIENT SCRIPTURES AND THE MODERN JEW," ETC.

Eugene, Oregon

Wipf and Stock Publishers
199 West 8th Avenue, Suite 3
Eugene, Oregon 97401

The Shepherd of Israel and His Scattered Flock
A Solution of the Enigma of Jewish History
By Baron, David
ISBN: 1-59244-607-8
Publication date 3/17/2004
Previously published by Morgan and Scott, 1910

PREFACE

THIS book is primarily a continuous exposition of a very important scripture which briefly but very graphically depicts Israel's present state among the nations, and looks on prophetically to God's dealings with them in the future.

The summary of Jewish history, which might almost stand by itself, and which some readers may perhaps regard as not the least valuable portion of the work, is included chiefly in order to confirm and elucidate the Scripture, and to show how truly the Word of God has been fulfilled in the history of this unique people.

Of the importance of this subject, especially in these days of unsettlement and doubt, I need not here speak. Christians, as stated in the book itself, have reason to be thankful for the confirmation of Scripture, and for the light thrown on its pages by recent historical and monumental discoveries ; but, after all, the most eloquent monument to the faithfulness of God and to the everlasting truth of His holy Word is the JEW ; and there is an inscription more striking and legible than any which can be found written on papyrus or graven on rock— an inscription nearly twenty centuries long, consisting of the history of the Jewish nation since their dispersion, written for the most part in their own blood, and which supplies more light upon, and confirmation of, God's living oracles, than can be obtained from any other source except within the Bible itself.

But this is not primarily an apologetic or argumentative book. Much rather have I sought, by God's help, not only to point out the true solution of the enigma of the history of the nation to which I have the honour to belong, and which I love, not less, but more, since by the grace of God I have been led to recognise in Christ Israel's true Shepherd and King ; but I have tried also to keep before me the spiritual profit of my readers, whether Jews or Christians.

One or two further explanations are perhaps necessary. The summary of Jewish history among the Christian nations is derived from various standard Jewish and Christian sources, as indicated in the footnotes ; but I must specially acknowledge my indebtedness to the recently-published *Geschichte des Jüdischen Volkes seit der Zerstörung Jerusalems*, by Professor F. Heman, of Basel, the most important and most impartial history of the Jewish people since the destruction of the second Temple which has yet appeared, and which, it is to be hoped, will before long be made accessible to English readers.

In reference to this section of the book, some may remark that it presents only the tragic side of the story of this undying race. But though it is true that the life of Israel through the Middle

PREFACE

Ages was not quite " an unbroken horror of carnage and rapine," and that " there were spells of respite, some of them fairly long, during which the Jews were permitted to live and grow fat " ; these sabbaths of rest, as the same writer truly proceeds to state, " can be likened not inaptly to the periods during which a prudent husbandman suffers his land to lie fallow, in the hope of a richer harvest. They are only intervals between the acts of a tedious and bloody tragedy, with a continent for its stage, and seven centuries for its night."

The other elements which go to make up Jewish history since the dispersion—the development of the Rabbinic system and its effects on Jewish character—the social life, and manners and customs of the Jews, of which the synagogue might be said to be the emblem and centre—concerns more *inner* Judaism ; and, though an acquaintance with them is of importance to the student and specialist, they are not of equal interest to the general reader. It would, moreover, be outside the scope of this modest work to enter into these details. For the same reason I have omitted all reference to that part of the Jewish nation whose lot has been cast among Mohammedan and heathen peoples ; not only because they have for many centuries formed a very inconsiderable minority of the Diaspora, as compared with the masses of their brethren in Christendom, but because they have played no special *rôle* in the world's history, nor have they in any perceptible degree influenced the destiny of the peoples among whom they lived. If the physical suffering which they endured has been less intense than that to which Israel has been subject in Europe, the scorn and contempt to which they were with few exceptions exposed, from races much inferior to themselves, has been if anything greater, and, intellectually and morally, they are on a lower grade than their brethren who are scattered in European countries.

For the copying and translation of longer and shorter passages from German sources, as well as in sifting the facts in the historic summary generally, I am indebted to the able and diligent pen of my dear wife, who has so truly been a fellow-worker with me for the Kingdom of God these past twenty-seven years.

Finally, I would beg my reader to note, in reference to the Scriptures dealt with, that while the whole psalm which forms the basis of my subject, and which stands at the commencement, has been copied from the Revised Version, in the exposition itself I have not been bound to any translation, but have had the Hebrew text before me.

It is the prayer of my heart that at least in some little way these pages may conduce to the glory of the great Shepherd of Israel and to the blessing of His long-scattered and suffering flock, concerning which He has still wonderful purposes of grace, and thoughts of salvation.

DAVID BARON.

CONTENTS

CHAP.		PAGE
	PREFACE	v
	INTRODUCTORY	1
	THE DIVISION	5
I.	THE INVOCATION	7
II.	ISRAEL'S WOES DEPICTED	14
III.	A SUMMARY OF JEWISH HISTORY SINCE THE DESTRUCTION OF THE SECOND TEMPLE	25
	A. The National Catastrophe	25
	B. The Final Struggle with Imperial Rome	27
	C. Degradation and Sufferings heaped upon the Jews by the Papal Church	28
	D. Jewish Sufferings in the Middle Ages	36
	E. The Jews in France	37
	F. The Jews in England	42
	G. The Fiery Furnace in Germany	46
	H. The Jewish Tragedy in Spain and Portugal	52
	I. The Jews in Poland	69
	J. The Reformation and Since	72

CONTENTS

CHAP.		PAGE
IV.	THE PRIMARY CAUSE OF JEWISH SUFFERINGS: ISRAEL A PROPHET OF JUDGMENT	80
V.	ISRAEL'S SUFFERINGS IN FULFILMENT OF DIVINE FORECASTS AND AN OBJECT-LESSON TO CHRISTENDOM	93
VI.	THE PARABLE OF THE VINE: THE CONTRAST BETWEEN THE PAST AND THE PRESENT	103
VII.	"TURN AGAIN, WE BESEECH THEE"	112
VIII.	THE REFRAIN	117

APPENDICES

I.	WERE THE JEWS JUSTIFIED IN REJECTING JESUS OF NAZARETH?	125
II.	HEBREW CHRISTIAN TESTIMONY TO ISRAEL	129

GIVE ear, O Shepherd of Israel,
Thou that leadest Joseph like a flock;
Thou that sittest upon the cherubim, shine forth.
Before Ephraim and Benjamin and Manasseh, stir up thy might,
And come to save us.
Turn us again, O God;
And cause thy face to shine, and we shall be saved.

O LORD GOD of hosts,
How long wilt thou be angry against the prayer of thy people?
Thou hast fed them with the bread of tears,
And given them tears to drink in large measure.
Thou makest us a strife unto our neighbours:
And our enemies laugh among themselves.
Turn us again, O God of hosts;
And cause thy face to shine, and we shall be saved.

Thou broughtest a vine out of Eygpt:
Thou didst drive out the nations, and plantedst it.
Thou preparedst room before it,
And it took deep root, and filled the land.
The mountains were covered with the shadow of it,
And the boughs thereof were like cedars of God.
She sent out her branches unto the sea,
And her shoots unto the River.
Why hast thou broken down her fences,
So that all they which pass by the way do pluck her?
The boar out of the wood doth ravage it,
And the wild beasts of the field feed on it.

Turn again, we beseech thee, O God of hosts:
Look down from heaven, and behold, and visit this vine,
And the stock which thy right hand hath planted,
And the branch which thou madest strong for thyself.
It is burned with fire, it is cut down :
They perish at the rebuke of thy countenance.
Let thy hand be upon the man of thy right hand,
Upon the son of man whom thou madest strong for thyself.
So shall we not go back from thee.
Quicken thou us, and we will call upon thy name.
Turn us again, O LORD GOD of hosts:
Cause thy face to shine, and we shall be saved.
                                            (PSALM LXXX.)

INTRODUCTORY

THIS Psalm, about the Shepherd of Israel and His erring flock, is one of the most striking and comprehensive scriptures in the Bible ; it has reference to the past, present, and yet future dealings of God with the people whom He has chosen for the express purpose that in and through them " His way " might become known on all the earth, and " His saving health " among all nations. As I take up my pen to write out an exposition of it, my heart goes out in prayer that the same Holy Spirit who first inspired the prophetic writer to utter this sacred oracle may also illumine and guide and help His servant in the attempt to unfold it, so that my readers —whether Jews or Christians—may be constrained to give glory to God, and exclaim with Israel's great law-giver :

> "The Rock !
> His work is perfect ;
> For all His ways are judgment :
> A God of truth [or faithfulness], and without iniquity,
> Just and right is He."

INTRODUCTORY

I must touch only very briefly in passing on the question of date and origin; "definiteness" with regard to which (as is generally admitted by almost all commentators) "is unattainable." Some commentators suppose this psalm to have been originally a prayer of Judah for their brethren of the Northern Kingdom, after the latter were carried away captive by Shalmaneser into Assyria; because the only tribes mentioned in the invocation are Ephraim, Manasseh, and Benjamin, the greater part of which also joined with those tribes which broke away from the house of David, while part remained with Judah. Probability is supposed to be added to this view by the fact that in the Septuagint the words ὑπερ του Ασσυριου ("concerning the Assyrian") are added to the inscription which forms the title, and may be taken as an indication that the translators of that version, in the third or early in the second century before Christ, have regarded it as primarily a prayer for those who had been carried away into Assyria. But there is another, and to my mind a truer, explanation why these tribes are specially named.

There are in this psalm touching allusions to Israel's past history, and particularly to the wonders connected with the Exodus and the journey through the wilderness; when, with the cloud of glory—which subsequently "dwelt between the Cherubim"—and the pillar of fire, He led His people "like a flock," till the "vine" which He brought "out of Egypt," was safely planted on the promised holy soil, where it took root and flourished. Now, in that memorable march of God

INTRODUCTORY

at the head of His people from Egypt to Canaan, the three tribes which walked immediately in rear of the Tabernacle, with which the symbols of Jehovah's special presence in their midst were connected, were "Ephraim, Benjamin, and Manasseh" (Num. ii. 17—22); and as this psalm is an inspired prophetic prayer that, in keeping with His theocratic relation to them, God might once again come and take His place at the head of His people, and bring them out of a greater bondage than that of Egypt, and through this greater and more terrible wilderness than that of Sinai, therefore—in keeping with the historic foreground—these three tribes are especially named.

But whatever may have been the time and circumstances which occasioned its original composition, whatever the historic foreground to which it had but a very partial reference, there can be no doubt that the Spirit of God, who inspired its utterance, has preserved for us in the 80th psalm a permanent picture of Israel's woeful condition when banished from God's presence and scattered among the nations; while in the fervent cry for help in the invocation and in the thrice repeated refrain, which contains the real theme and fundamental prayer of this psalm, we have also a prophecy as to *how* and *whence* Israel's final deliverance and full salvation will yet come.

To repeat, then, this psalm is a prophetic prayer which shall yet ascend from the heart and soul of the godly remnant of Israel on behalf of the whole nation at the time of the end. But till

INTRODUCTORY

then—until the Spirit of Grace and of Supplication is poured out on Israel, and they learn to pray in the name of Him through whom alone their prayer shall be heard—it is well pleasing to God that Christians, whose privilege it is to be "watchmen on the walls of Zion," should pray for them after the manner, and more especially in the spirit, of this inspired model prayer ; and let me assure the reader that in seeking to lift up holy hands of intercession on behalf of this people, who, in spite of all, are still "beloved" of God "for the fathers' sakes," he himself shall be blessed.

THE DIVISION

THE whole psalm is divided into three unequal parts by the thrice repeated refrain:

"Turn us again, O God,
And cause Thy face to shine, and we shall be saved";

the first section consisting of the first three verses form the Invocation; in the second (verses 4—7) Israel's present unspeakably sad condition is graphically depicted, and used as the ground for the earnest cry for God's interposition on their behalf; and in the last and longest section (verses 8—19) the appeal to the Covenant God of the fathers is based on the ground of His former mercies to them.

CHAPTER I

THE INVOCATION

"O SHEPHERD of Israel, give ear"—this is the order of the words in the original in the first line of our psalm. How beautiful and significant is this name of God! It was first used by Jacob in blessing Ephraim and Manasseh in Gen. xlviii. 15: "The God before whom my fathers Abraham and Isaac did walk, *the God who hath fed me*"[1] (literally "who hath shepherded me") "all my life long unto this day, the Angel which hath redeemed me from all evil, bless the lads"; and again in his final blessing of Joseph he exclaims: "*Thence is the Shepherd the stone of Israel.*" We can imagine how full of meaning that name, as applied to God, must have been in the mouth of the patriarch. He knew what it meant to be a shepherd. For twenty years he had tended Laban's sheep, enduring all sorts of hardships and privations in his devotion to them. "Thus I was," he says in his remon-

[1] There is much more in the Hebrew word רעה than "to feed." There are implied in it also the ideas of keeping, leading, ruling over, &c.

strance with his wily father-in-law, " in the day the drought consumed me, and the frost by night; and my sleep departed from my eyes" (Gen. xxxi. 40). It subsequently became a very favourite name for God; and no wonder, for next to the precious names "father" and "husband," there is no name which so fully describes what God is to His people and to the soul that trusts in Him. It is, however, only in and through Christ that we can learn to know God in this very blessed relationship. This is clearly set forth in the prophetic scriptures in the Old Testament as well as in the New Testament. The great Old Testament scripture which sets forth the shepherd relation of God to His people is Ezekiel xxxiv. There we read how God will "seek" and "deliver" and "heal" and "strengthen" and "feed" and "rest" and "satisfy" His flock; but when we come to the last part of that chapter, He tells us that He would be and shall yet be all this for Israel *in and through the Messiah:* "*And I will set up one Shepherd over them,*" He says, and "*He shall feed them, even My servant David; He shall feed them and be their Shepherd; they shall dwell safely in the wilderness and sleep in the woods.*" And so also in the 37th chapter of the same prophet: "*And my servant David*[1] *shall be king over them, and*

---

[1] Even the Jews explained the name "David" in these passages as applying to the Messiah—the great Son of David, in whom all the promises to the Davidic house are centred. Thus Kimchi, in his comment on Ezek. xxxiv. 23, says: "My servant David—that is, the Messiah who shall spring from his

THE SHEPHERD OF ISRAEL 9

they all shall have one Shepherd; they shall also walk in My judgments and observe My statutes and do them." It is only, therefore, when Israel's ear is opened to hear the voice of Him who says, " I am the Good Shepherd : the Good Shepherd layeth down His life for the sheep," that they will be able intelligently and in truth to say, " Jehovah is my Shepherd " ; or to cry out, as the prophetic writer by the Spirit of Inspiration does in this psalm, " O Shepherd of Israel."

The figure of the Shepherd and the flock is continued in the second line :

"Thou that leddest Joseph like a flock"—

who in thy capacity as Shepherd of Israel didst tend and guide, and wert all to them that a shepherd is to his flock :

"*Thou that dwellest* [literally 'that sittest enthroned'] *between the Cherubim* "—

i.e., who didst manifest Thy special presence in our midst, dwelling in the Tabernacle and in the Temple in that symbolic cloud of the Shekinah glory—

"Shine forth"—

let the light of Thy countenance, O thou Sun of Righteousness, break through and dispel the clouds

seed in the time of salvation" ; and in the 24th verse of chapter xxxvii. he observes : " The King Messiah—His name shall be called David because He shall be of the seed of David." And so practically all the Jewish commentators.

and the darkness by which we are now surrounded.

But the word which the psalmist uses really expresses a prayer for the manifest and personal appearing of His glory for the deliverance of His oppressed, suffering people, and to the dismay of their enemies. It is a somewhat parallel cry to that in Isa. lxiv. 1, 2.

> "Oh that Thou wouldst rend the heavens, that Thou wouldst come down, that the mountains might quake at Thy presence . . . to make Thy Name known to Thine adversaries, that the nations may tremble at Thy presence."

In the Hebrew Psalter this word is found only three times, and in every case it is used in relation to the future personal, visible appearing and interposition of God on behalf of Israel and Zion. Its first use is in Psalm l. 2 :

> "Out of Zion, the perfection of beauty,
> God hath shined forth";

which is explained by the words which immediately follow :

> "Our God cometh, and shall not keep silence."

The second place is in Psalm lxxx. 1 ; and the third in Psalm xciv. 1 :

> "O Jehovah, thou God to whom vengeance belongeth,
> O God to whom vengeance belongeth, *shine forth.*"

And all these three passages in the Psalms are based on the sublime scripture in Deut.

THE BREAKING OF THE DAWN

xxxiii., in the blessing wherewith Moses, the man of God, blessed the children of Israel before he died.

"And he said:
 Jehovah came from Sinai,
 And rose [or "burst forth"—*i.e.*, as the rising sun] from Seir unto them;
 He *shined forth* from Mount Paran,
 And he came with [or "from"] the myriads of His holy ones:
 From His right hand went forth a fiery law unto them."

The imagery of this passage is beautiful, the figure being borrowed from the breaking of the dawn, and the progressive splendour of the sun-rising. Oh, what a wonderful event in the history of the world and of Israel was the revelation of the glory of Jehovah on Sinai! What a bursting forth of light on the moral darkness of this earth! But, alas! by reason of the weakness of the flesh it was not the light of life, but rather of death; for it revealed to man his sin and utter helplessness, and the perfect holiness of the God who is "a consuming fire."

But the law contained not only the promise, but was in itself also a preparation for the Gospel; and, therefore, in the fulness of time, though not attended by outward splendour as on Sinai, another Epiphany (2 Tim. i. 10) of God our Saviour took place, bringing not "a fiery law," but the Gospel of His grace, which abolished death and brought life and immortality to light. The acceptable year of the Lord ushered in by that Epiphany is rapidly running to its close; and although for nigh nineteen centuries favour has been preached to the wicked, yet he has not learned righteousness. Men are beginning to ask if the faith founded by the Son of God has not already proved a failure; and scoffers boldly say: "Where is the promise of His coming, and what sign is there of any change or interruption of the present state of things?" Even the professing Church, lost for the most part in worldliness and error, seeks to strike its roots in the earth, crying peace and progress, and acting as if all things will for ever continue as they are.[1]

But this earth shall yet again see the glory of the personal presence of the Lord, and the answer to the prophetic prayer, "Shine forth," will be the "appearing of the glory of our great God and Saviour, Jesus Christ"—"at the revelation of the Lord Jesus from heaven, with the angels of His power, in flaming fire, rendering vengeance to them that know not God, and to them that obey not the Gospel of our Lord Jesus Christ" (Titus ii. 13; 2 Thess. i. 7, 8)—when in a special manner He will show Himself to be the "Shepherd of Israel" and their Deliverer.

The prayer is continued in the same strain in the second verse:

"Before Ephraim and Benjamin and Manasseh,"

—even as Thou didst in our fathers' times when

[1] See the chapter, "The Silence of God—how it shall be Broken," in the author's work, *The Ancient Scriptures and the Modern Jew*.

Thou didst march at the head of the tribes, in the Pillar of Cloud and Pillar of Fire, scattering Thine enemies before Thee [1]—

"Stir up Thy might,"

which now seems to be slumbering; and which reminds us of Isa. li. 9: "Awake, awake, put on strength, O Arm of Jehovah; awake as in the days of old, the generations of ancient times. Art Thou not it [that great power] that cut Rahab [*i.e.*, Egypt] in pieces, that pierced the dragon [of the Nile—*i.e.*, Pharaoh]? Art Thou not it which dried up the sea, the waters of the great deep; that made the depths of the sea a way for the redeemed to pass over?" Oh that Thou wouldst again "stir up Thy might and come to save us!" or, as the last line of the second verse of our psalm reads more literally, "And go forth for salvation to us," which prayer for God's *Yeshuah* ("salvation") will only be fulfilled in the going or coming forth of Him whose Hebrew name *is* ישוע *Jeshua—i.e.*, "Saviour," and who shall yet "save His people from their sins" (Matt. i. 21), and "out of all their troubles" (Psa. xxv. 22).

---

[1] See remarks on the reason of the special mention of these tribes in the Introduction.

CHAPTER II

ISRAEL'S WOES DEPICTED

WE come now to the consideration of the second section, in which, as already stated, Israel's present very woeful condition is depicted and used as the plea for God's interposition and deliverance:

"O Jehovah God of Tzebaoth,
   How long wilt Thou be angry [lit. 'wilt Thou smoke']
      against the prayer of Thy people?
   Thou hast fed them with the bread of tears,
   And given them tears to drink in large measure,[1]
   Thou makest us a strife [or 'a subject of contention'] unto
      our neighbours:
   And our enemies laugh among themselves."

Now, in reading these lines, which so truly and graphically summarise the experience of the Jewish

---

[1] The word *shalish* means literally "the third part" (of some large measure). It is found elsewhere only in Isa. xl. 12, where it is rendered in the Authorised and Revised Versions simply "a measure." The "measure" is probably the Ephah, the third part of which, as Delitzsch observes, though puny for the dust of the earth, is "a large measure for tears."

people for so many centuries, we are first of all reminded of the fact that the Great Shepherd of Israel had purposed and provided something very different for His flock. Oh, there are green pastures prepared "upon the mountains of Israel" (Ezek. xxxiv. 14); there are "the waters of quietness" (Psa. xxiii. 2) flowing from "wells of salvation," from which they might drink and be satisfied. How is it, then, that Israel has now to eat the bread of tears, and have tears in great measure for his drink? For an answer to this important question we need go no farther than the very next Psalm. It is not without design that the 81st Psalm immediately follows the 80th; for it supplies the explanation and answer to the "How long?" (ver. 4) and the "Why?" (ver. 12) contained in it. The reason of Israel's special sorrows is found in his peculiar relationship to Jehovah. The God of heaven condescended to enter into a special national covenant with this people when he brought them out of the land of bondage. Great and wonderful blessings were promised to them if they were "good and obedient" (Isa. i. 19). This is how God solemnly charged and warned them:

> "Hear, O My people, and I will testify unto thee;
> O Israel, if thou wouldst but hearken unto Me!
> There shall no strange god be in thee;
> Neither shalt thou worship any strange god.
> I am Jehovah thy God,
> Who brought thee up out of the land of Egypt.
> Open thy mouth wide and I will fill it."

ISRAEL'S WOES DEPICTED

What He was ready to feed and satisfy them with He tells us in the last verse of that psalm:

> "He should have fed them also with the fat of the wheat,
> With honey out of the rock, should I satisfy thee."

> "Oh that My people *would* hearken unto Me,"

He exclaims in yearning desire over them—

> "That Israel *would* walk in my ways!"

"but"—He sorrowfully laments in the eleventh verse—

> "My people hearkened not to My voice,
> And Israel would none of Me.'

Oh, how much there is included in this eleventh verse of the 81st psalm: "*My people hearkened not: Israel would none of Me!*"—it summarises Israel's many transgressions, their stubborn unbelief and innumerable provocations of the Most High. Shall I stop to trace the beginning, progress, and climax of Israel's disobedience and progressive apostasy? The first stage downwards was the disregard of the most solemn charge: "There shall no strange god be in thee; neither shalt thou worship any strange god"—which contains the keynote of the revelation given from Sinai, and the fundamental command of the decalogue.

I do not wish to dwell much on this point here, having already elsewhere [1] pointed out the very

See *A Divine Forecast of Jewish History.*

PRONENESS TO IDOLATRY

humbling object-lesson which Jewish history presents in this respect to all the rest of mankind, and how it contradicts all the boasted assertions of human progress and development in relation to things spiritual and eternal.

Modern so-called "progressive" Rabbis—confirmed and supported by many "modern" Christian theologians, who also no longer believe in a Divine revelation—speak boastfully as if the Jews had discovered or *evolved* the belief in One God. "This," says one of the greatest of modern Jewish lights (viz., that the Jewish people "created Monotheism out of itself"), "is Israel's imperishable merit."[1] But the very opposite is the truth. Not only did Israel not create the belief in one true and living God "out of itself," but history testifies to the fact that Israel was naturally as prone to idolatry as any of the other Semitic peoples to whom they are related; and when left to themselves they could not even *retain* the knowledge of the living God after it had been divinely communicated to them. And if the light of the knowledge of God *was* maintained in their midst, the fact is to be ascribed, not to the "monotheistic genius" of the Jewish people, but to Divine acts and interpositions, in judgments and in mercy, of Israel's God. Instead of claiming "imperishable

---

[1] "Es hat den Monotheismus in gewaltigem 'Ringen mit Gott und Menschen', wie die Bibel sagt, aus sich geschaffen. Das ist Israel's unvergängliches Verdienst"—*Das Judenthum*, by Dr. M. Güdemann, Chief Rabbi of Vienna (p. 17); the edition from which I am translating was published in Vienna by R. Löwit in 1902.

merit," as is done by modern Rabbis, Israel's true prophets and psalmists confess with broken hearts that "to us belongeth confusion of face, to our kings, to our princes, and to our fathers" (Dan. ix. 8); for though the God of Glory revealed Himself in our midst, and dealt with us as with no other nation, "though He commanded the clouds from above and opened the doors of heaven and rained down manna upon them to eat," and showed them many other great and wonderful signs, "their hearts were not right with Him," and they continuously "turned back and dealt unfaithfully like their fathers; they were turned aside like a deceitful bow. *For they provoked Him to anger with their high places, and moved Him to jealousy with their graven images*" (Psa. lxxviii. 23, 24, 57, 58).

This was the beginning and the first stage in Israel's national apostasy—the turning from God to idols. The climax was reached when, after a long-continued process of disobedience and self-hardening, and because their hearts were already alienated from God, Israel turned their backs upon Him who is "the brightness of God's glory and the express image of His person." The Scribes and Pharisees in Christ's time, and the majority of the Jews of the present day, would have us believe that they rejected Jesus of Nazareth because He wanted to mislead and turn them away from God and His holy law. Many of them in their ignorance sincerely believed and still believe this to be the case. But, alas! this very ignorance is part of

WHY ISRAEL REJECTED CHRIST

the awful consequences of Israel's prior alienation from their heavenly Father, and from the true spirit of Moses and the prophets. No: Israel rejected Christ, not because He went counter to, or sought in any way to lead them astray from, God, or because His teaching was contradictory to the Law and to the testimony which was already in their hands; but because, on the contrary, He sought to bring them back to God, and was Himself the very image of God, who as the only true Israelite, not only bore witness to the law and the prophets, but Himself *magnified* the Law, and fulfilled and exemplified it in His own life. How pathetic is the Gospel narrative in this respect! The self-deceived leaders of the people sought to justify their hostility to Jesus and their rejection of His claim on the ground of their zeal for God. "We have one Father, even God," they said. But Jesus said unto them, "If God were your Father, *ye would love Me;* for I proceeded forth and came from God; neither came I of myself, but He sent Me" (John viii. 41, 42). Again, they put it on the ground of their zeal for the Law; but His answer was, These very Scriptures which ye search, and for which ye profess such zeal, are "they *which testify of Me*." "Had ye believed Moses, ye would have believed Me, for he wrote of Me; it is written in the prophets, And they shall be all taught of God. *Every man, therefore, that hath heard, and hath learned of the Father, cometh unto Me*" (John v. 39—47; vi. 45).[1]

[1] See Appendix I.—"Were the Jews Justified in Rejecting Jesus of Nazareth?"

In the light of the Gospel narrative and the history of Israel's dealings with, and their attitude to, their Messiah, how solemn and full of significance is God's complaint:

> "But My people hearkened not to My voice;
> And Israel would none of Me!"

for in the rejection of Christ and in their resistance of the Spirit, Israel reached the climax of their progressive apostasy from their God.

The sad and terrible consequence of it all is tersely set forth in the twelfth verse of the 81st Psalm:

> "So I gave them up unto their own hearts' lust,
> And they walked in their own counsels."

So the Authorised Version reads: but the words in the original are much more forcible and striking, literally:

> "So [or then] I *sent them forth* [or 'cast them out'] in the stubbornness of their heart:
> Let them walk [or 'they shall walk'] in their own counsels."

This is the most terrible thing which can befall any man or nation—when God says, "Ephraim is joined to idols, let him alone" (Hosea iv. 17), or in the words of personified Wisdom:

> "They would none of my counsel;
> They despised all my reproof;
> Therefore shall they eat of the fruit of their own way,
> And be filled with their own devices" (Prov. i. 30, 31).

THE NIGHT OF WEEPING

"So He sent them forth." It reminds us of the very solemn words of Hosea ix. 17 : "My God will cast them away, because they did not hearken unto Him ; and they shall be wanderers among the nations."

And with this banishment from God's presence, and their dispersion among the nations, began Israel's night of weeping. What a long and dark night it has been to them ! How terribly real and true have the words proved to be :

> "Thou hast fed them with the bread of tears,
> And given them tears to drink in large measure" !

What other people under heaven have suffered and wept so much as the Jews?

At the inauguration of Israel's great and many national tribulations—at the very commencement of the prophetic period called "the times of the Gentiles"—Jeremiah, who was an eye-witness of the calamities which fell on his people at the fall of Jerusalem and the destruction of the first Temple by the Chaldeans, which marked the close of the first stage of Israel's apostasy and punishment, exclaims : "Is it nothing to you, all ye that pass by? Behold and see if there be any sorrow like unto my sorrow, which is done unto me ; wherewith Jehovah hath afflicted me in the day of His fierce anger." And some five and a half centuries later, after the second stage of Israel's national sin culminated in the rejection of Christ, which brought about the breaking-up of their national polity, and inaugurated the longer and more terrible captivity than the seventy years' exile in Babylon, the historian Josephus, in commencing to write the history of *The Jewish Wars*, and particularly the final desperately heroic, but futile, death struggle with the great Roman world-power, says in his Preface: "Accordingly it appears to me that the misfortunes of all men from the beginning of the world, if they be compared with those of the Jews, are not so considerable as they were . . . this makes it impossible for me to contain my lamentations."

This was at the very beginning of our "Christian Era." What would that historian have said if he could have foreseen the untold woes and miseries which have been heaped upon this people in the nineteen centuries which have intervened? As I write, there lies before me a rare book, written in the middle of the sixteenth century by the Jewish Rabbi and physician, Joseph ha-Kohen, who was born in Avignon in 1496, but was driven by persecution to Italy, where he died in 1575. It is a history of his people from the destruction of the second Temple down to his time. And what do you think is the title of the book? "*Emek ha-Baca—* 'the Valley of Tears.'" And the name, as he truly observes in his Preface, accurately describes its contents. "For everyone," he says, "who will read it must do it with astonishment" (and as a Christian I must add also with *shame* and *indignation*) "in his heart, and as the tears stream down from his eyes, he will be constrained to exclaim, 'How long, O Lord; how long!'" It is one long martyrology, the record of an almost

THE VALLEY OF TEARS 23

unbroken chain of unparalleled sufferings—a chronicle of massacres, oppressions, banishments, fiendish tortures, spoliations and degradations, which have been inflicted upon the Jews for the most part by so-called Christian nations. No wonder that another Jewish historian in Italy (Samuel Usque), who wrote a work in Portuguese also early in the sixteenth century [1] depicting the universal misery of his people, exclaims in his Introduction : " To which part of the world shall I turn to find healing for my wound, forgetfulness for my pain, and comfort for my heavy, unbearable sufferings? Among the riches and enjoyments of happy Asia I find myself a heavy-laden pilgrim. In sun-burnt Africa, rich with gold, I am a wretched, starving exile. And thou, Europe, my hell upon earth ! What shall I say about thee? How shall I praise thee, vicious, warring Italy? Like a hungry lion hast thou fed on the torn flesh of my lambs ! Ye corrupted French meadows, poisoned grass did my lambs eat on you ! Proud, barbaric, mountainous Germany, thou hast thrown down and broken to pieces my young men from the top of thine Alps ! Ye sweet and fresh waters of England, bitter and salt draughts did my flock drink of you ! Hypocritical, cruel, and blood-thirsty Spain, ravenous hungry wolves have devoured and are still devouring my flock in thy midst. . . . *It is the lot of every creature to experience change;*

[1] The title of the work is *Consolaçao as Tribulaçoens de Israel*. I am translating the abstract from Professor Heman's new and important work *Die Geschichte des Jüdischen Volkes*, pp. 303, 304.

but with Israel it is not so: his misfortune never changes, his sorrows never end." "All peoples of the earth," laments yet another Jewish author, Joseph Ibn Verga, in the middle of the sixteenth century, "are as one in their hatred against the Jews; all creatures in heaven and on earth are united in sworn hostility to them. Before the Jewish child can lisp, it is already followed or surrounded by hatred and scorn. We are despised as the lowest worms."

To show that this is no mere hyperbole nor rhetoric, but literally true, I beg the reader to follow me in a summary of Jewish history among the so-called Christian nations, which—though it may form a long break in the continuous exposition of the scripture which we are considering—I feel myself constrained to include, because of the general lack of knowledge of the history of the scattered people since the destruction of the second Temple, and also because of the absence of any really satisfactory work in the English language on this most important subject.

CHAPTER III

A SUMMARY OF JEWISH HISTORY SINCE THE DESTRUCTION OF THE SECOND TEMPLE

A. The National Catastrophe.

"NOT one stone remained upon another; the Temple and city lay in smoking ruins. The foundations of the Temple terraces alone withstood destruction, and of the great and glorious city Titus left standing only the three strong towers which bore the names of Hyppicus, Mariamne, and Phasael; all beside were ashes and heaps of ruins. During the course of the long siege more than a million of people had perished in the city; thousands had fallen in battles in the country. Those who fell into the hands of the Romans and were not slain were sold into slavery, the fate of all prisoners in the olden time. Many thousands went forth to the mines and quarries of Egypt; other thousands were bought by the slave dealers at absurd prices; all the markets were glutted with Jewish slaves. Thousands more were shared as spoil by the conquerors and sent as presents to their friends; the finest and most powerful of the men and youths were selected for conflicts with wild beasts, for gladiatorial games, and to grace the triumphal train of the Emperor and Cæsar; 900,000 of the sons and daughters of Zion thus witnessed in all the world to the destruction of the Jewish kingdom and nation.

"In every city through which Titus passed on his return to Rome splendid entertainments in honour of his victory were celebrated, at which hundreds of Jewish youths were compelled to fight with one another, and with wild beasts, till death. His triumphal car to Rome was drawn by seven hundred beautiful youths in chains, among whom were the two last bravest party leaders, John of Gischala and Simon bar-Giora, who had fallen alive into the hands of the Romans; after these were borne the most precious of the spoils from the Temple—vessels and treasure, the great golden candlesticks, the golden table, and the precious sacred Roll of the Law.

"Coins were struck memorialising the fall of Judah, and the splendid triumphal arch of Titus still shows the captive Jews in chains, and the sacred vessels of their sanctuary. While almost all other memorials of Rome's victories have long since fallen into ruin, this monument of Jewish misery, like the Jewish people itself, remains to-day a wonderful coincidence in the history of the world! And which will endure the longest—the misery of the Jewish captivity or its memorial?"[1]

[1] Heman, *Geschichte des Jüdischen Volkes.*

B. The Final Struggle with Imperial Rome.

This overthrow of the Jewish nation seemed irreparable and final; but some sixty years later the bitter struggle with the power of Rome commenced anew, and the desperate courage of the Jews and their overwhelming numbers protracted the contest three and a half years. The Emperor Hadrian had revived a law by which the practice of circumcision was punishable by death; he also proposed to build a city over the ruins of Jerusalem, to be named Ælia Capitolina, and to erect on the platform foundation of the destroyed Temple of Jehovah a temple for the worship of Jupiter. This maddened the Jews, threatening as it did to destroy both their separate national existence and their national hopes—ever expectant of the coming of Messiah and of future glory in their land. The appearance of a man at this time, who claimed to be the promised Messiah, and whom the great Rabbi Akiba hailed as such by the name of Bar Cochba ("Son of a Star"),[1] in allusion to the prophecy of Balaam, inflamed their zeal to white heat. The Rabbis and students of the Law ardently encouraged the revolt. The numbers who rallied to Bar Cochba are reported by Dio Cassius as 580,000, including some hired soldiery. For some two years their fierce valour caused Tinius Rufus, the Roman Governor, to retreat before them; the additional help in troops sent from Rome was insufficient to cope with the

[1] After the bitter disappointment of their hopes the survivors changed the name to Bar Coziba ("Son of a Lie").

Jewish forces, madly confident of success, until Julius Severus, the most capable of all Roman generals of the time, was recalled from Britain. The task of subduing the Jews was no light one even for him; it was a prolonged guerilla warfare, the foes not to be met in open conflict, but having to be sought out in their places of concealment, incurring terrible suffering and waste of life to both armies.

The last stand was made at Bithar, which held out two years, till the people were reduced to starvation; it is probable also that treachery aided the Romans in the end. All the men were put to the sword, and the women and children reserved for slavery.

Five hundred and eighty thousand Jews are said to have perished in battle, beside those who perished by famine and sickness. " Judea was almost wholly a wilderness "; 50 castles and 285 villages were entirely destroyed. At the yearly market, by Abraham's Oak at Hebron, Jewish slaves were sold at a nominal price; a Jew was worth no more than a horse.

A Temple to Jupiter rose on Mount Moriah, and Jerusalem received the name of Ælia Capitolina; Jews being forbidden on pain of death to come within sight of the city.

C. Degradation and Sufferings heaped upon the Jews by the Papal Church.

It would be a weary task to give even a brief summary of the precarious conditions of

Jewish life under the pagan Roman emperors. We pass over nearly two hundred years in silence, and take up the thread of their history at a date when Christianity had become the State religion of the Roman Empire. For a brief three years the Emperor Constantine was tolerant of all religions, and the Jews enjoyed the same rights as other subjects, and their Rabbis the privileges granted to the leaders of the Christians and to heathen priests. In the year 315, however, a new decree was issued, declaring the Jews to be " an injurious, impious sect," which must be proscribed and repressed. The first Christian Council of which history takes cognisance, the Council of Nicæa, resolved to break those ties of relationship, the result of their common origin, which until now had existed to some extent between the Synagogue and the Church. Among other things, Easter was henceforth to be observed universally on a fixed date, independent of the Jewish calendar. Eusebius relates that the Emperor addressed the assembled bishops : " It seems unworthy of us to celebrate this holy festival after the custom of the Jews. We desire to have nothing in common with this so hated people, for the Redeemer has marked out another path for us. To this we will keep, and be free from disgraceful association with this people."

Thus did *the first Christian Council wholly forget the love of Christ,* and breathe out only hatred and enmity against the unhappy people of the Jews.

And these first " Christian " edicts were the

30 A SUMMARY OF JEWISH HISTORY

precursors of many passed by subsequent Councils, the one aim of which was to degrade and humble them, and to represent them in the eyes of the world as the offscouring and pariahs of mankind. The natural consequences soon followed. Marriages between Jews and Christians were made punishable by death; Jews were excluded from all public offices. Sometimes, indeed, the expensive *duties* of magistracy were laid upon them, while its exemptions and privileges were denied them. The evidence of Jews against Christians was declared inadmissible; for the Israelite was, in the eyes of the Christian of that period, worse than an infidel, and was designated in the official language of the Church *perfidus*—*i.e.*, a man to whom no faith or credit could be given; "*Oremus et pro perfides Judæis*" are the words of the Liturgy of Good Friday, and all the divines and canonists of the period used the expression.[1]

No Christian was to let or sell his house to a Jew. In one of the earliest Councils it was decreed that no Christian might eat with a Jew; and Chrysostom improved upon this ordinance by protesting that Christians ought not to hold *any* intercourse with Jews, "whose souls are the habitations of demons and whose synagogues are their playground."

A Jew might not sit in the presence of a priest; in a quarrel, if a Jew should strike a priest, death by fire, with the confiscation of his goods, was the penalty.

They were excluded from all schools, both higher

[1] Von Döllinger.

SHUT UP TO USURY

and lower. On Christian festivals Jews were not to be seen in the streets; so it was enacted in the Third and Fourth Councils of Orleans, "since their appearance would be a species of offence to Christianity."

At the Council of Vienna it was decreed that "no Jew should be admitted in a public bathing establishment, an inn, or a house of call for journeymen"—in short, the Jew was to be shunned "like one plague-stricken, whose very breath is infectious, like a dangerous seducer whose speech harbours the poison of scepticism and unbelief."[1]

Jews might not traffic nor practise any profession or handicraft: nor could they engage in agriculture, since the holding of land was forbidden them everywhere. They were *shut up* to money-lending and usury, which became an additional cause of their moral and physical ruin, since they were used only too often as a sponge in the hands of rulers, which could be wrung out when full, and then given over to the fury of the people.

The climax of Jewish hatred on the part of the Papal Church found expression in the Lateran Council of 1215. At this Council the whole of Western Christianity might be said to have been represented, for there were present at it: 71 archbishops, 412 bishops, 800 abbots, and a host of other Church dignitaries and priests. Its decrees were embodied in seventy canons, four of which deal with the Jews, and the one which has proved of the most terrible consequence to the scattered people in Europe for a number of centuries was

[1] Von Döllinger.

that which practically put upon them the badge of outlawry. Henceforth the Jews " in all Christendom and in all times " " were ordained to wear a distinctive dress or badge." This humiliating mark was soon placed upon the scattered people everywhere. In some lands it was a badge in shape of a wheel, red, yellow, or parti-coloured, fixed upon the breast; in others it was a square patch placed upon the shoulder, or hat. At Avignon the sign was a pointed yellow cap; at Prague a sleeve of the same colour; in Italy and Germany a horn-shaped head-dress, red or green, and so on.

"Thus," says Professor Heman, " were the Jews [by this badge of degradation] given over by the Church and the representatives of the Christian religion to shame and reproach for half a millennium."

And the worst consequences of this degrading position in which they were placed were that the Jews lost all self-respect and sense of their own dignity; they became outwardly obsequious in manner, and everywhere cringed in abject humility and slavishness of spirit; but at heart they became ever more and more embittered against Christians, and more intense in their hostility to Christianity. Utterly helpless in themselves, they were condemned by the leaders of Christianity to be the pariahs of mankind, and were compelled to endure contempt and hatred, plundering and banishment, blows and murder, from all the world. From this time especially the Jewish people became the martyr nation of the earth, and of mankind; and

DEGRADATION OF CHARACTER

its tormentors were the Christians, who behaved infinitely worse to them than the Mohammedans and heathen.

"The material loss which the Christians are supposed to have suffered in the course of centuries from the usury of the Jews, into which they were forced against their will, has been far outweighed by the loss of property, blood, and life, which the Jews have suffered since they were subjected to wear the yellow badge. But quite impossible to estimate is the injury to character suffered by the Jews as a result of this abominable outrage. The abject, slavish spirit, malicious craftiness, artful cunning, painful timidity, and all other faults of character which till lately have been made a reproach against them—these are all chargeable to the humiliating and scandalous treatment which they have received from Christians since the Lateran Council." [1]

Men wise before their age, and even those noted for Christian sanctity within the Papal Church, found no place in their hearts for compassion for this afflicted people. "It is true that here and there in the Dark Ages there was an occasional gleam of pity, or even of justice. It is to the lasting honour of Bernard of Clairvaux that during the whirling excitement of the Second Crusade he urged the soldiers of the Cross not to slaughter the people ' who were scattered among all nations as living memorials of Christ's passion.' And the illustrious Raymond Lull, who in the opening years of the fourteenth century died on the

Heman, *Geschichte des Jüdischen Volkes.*

African coast in the name and service of our blessed Redeemer, kneeling on the sand while the stones crashed around him, and crying with his last shaking breath, ' None but Christ ! None but Christ ! ' was the pioneer of Jewish missions." But Peter of Clugny, who was a contemporary of Bernard of Clairvaux, sought to incite Louis VII. of France to plunder the Jews, saying that the blaspheming Jews were worse than the Saracens ; and Thomas Aquinas advised Alice of Burgundy that the Jews were by their own guilt under sentence of perpetual slavery, and that the lords of the land had therefore the right to treat Jewish property as their own. The gentle Ambrose already in the fourth century designated burning synagogues in Rome by the mob " a work well pleasing to God," while a century later the pugilistic Christian bishop and father, Cyril of Alexandria, himself led a " Christian " mob against the Jewish quarter of that imperial city ; demolished their synagogues, pillaged their dwellings, and hounded the inmates out of the city in which they had lived and prospered for seven centuries. " Forty thousand of them, the most industrious and thrifty part of the population, were driven forth to join their brethren in exile."

As to the Popes, there are a few notable exceptions of some who shielded the Jews in their own States, chiefly, it must be confessed, because of their commercial enterprise and wealth, which were such important factors in mediæval Europe ; but most of the papal pontiffs, who were regarded not only as the heads of Christendom, but as the very

ATTITUDE OF POPES 35

"Vicars of Christ" on earth, were their relentless persecutors, and promulgated edicts which breathe fire and sword against the Jews. "Whenever in mediæval times a pope was consecrated the Hebrew congregation were among the attendants, standing with slavish gestures, full of fear or timid hope, while the Chief Rabbi at their head carried on his shoulders the mysterious veiled Roll of the Holy Law. They were accustomed to read their fate in the gloomy or genial countenance of the new pope. Was it to be toleration or oppression? While the Rabbi handed the Vicar of Christ the scroll for confirmation, their eyes scanned keenly the face that turned towards him. As the scroll was handed back, this was the formula which the Pope was accustomed to utter: "We recognise the Law, but we condemn the view of Judaism; for the Law is fulfilled through Christ, whom the blind people of Judah still expect as the Messiah." [1] "A deadly fright had overcome him," writes Pope Stephen VI. (885—91) to the Archbishop of Narbonne, "on hearing that the Jews there, those enemies of God, by royal grant, possessed allodial property, and that Christians dwelled together with these dogs, and even rendered them services, while by way of punishment for the death of Christ all grants and promises sworn by God Himself had been taken away"; while the declaration of Innocent III. that the whole nation was, for its guilt's sake, doomed by God to perpetual slavery, became the Magna Charta always appealed to by

[1] Hosmer, *The Jews*, in "The Story of the Nations" series.

all who thirsted for the possessions of the Jews and their gains.

D. Jewish Sufferings in the Middle Ages.

Turning from the un-Christian attitude of the spiritual guides and leaders of the Christian Church to the experience of the Jewish people at the hands of the princes and peoples of so-called Christian nations, what a terrible picture meets our gaze! " Jews Massacred in France," " Jews Massacred in Germany," " Jews Massacred in England," " Jews Massacred in Germany and France," " Jews Massacred in Spain," again and again and again. These headings, not to mention expulsions, oppressions, and spoliations without number, stare us in the face as we turn over the pages of the history of mediæval Europe, and the cold lines assume a terrible significance as we peruse tale after tale of bodily and mental torment, such as no other people have suffered and survived. And as we read on and try to realise the awful scenes, the desolate cry of the sufferers rings in our ears like a long-drawn wail borne across the centuries: " How long, O Lord, how long? "[1]

A few facts from their experience in the leading countries of Europe must suffice.

By confining the Jewish population in the narrow quarters of a ghetto whose space never widened, though the families within it increased, where they were shut within gates every night, they were

[1] G. F. Abbott, *Israel in Europe.*

kept like a caged beast who can be slaughtered at will ; and whenever necessity forced the Jew to go abroad the yellow badge at once marked him as an object for insult and violence.

A people held to be so degraded, so accursed, and of a double necessity living their life apart, even while dispersed among the other peoples, regarded with suspicion and continually exposed to violence ; without hope of justice, became suspicious, hated and avoided the sight of others, and appeared to justify the evil opinion formed of them. It was easy to make the hated people the scapegoat in all cases of crimes committed, and, in that superstitious and ignorant age, of evils also which had a natural origin.

"If sickness prevailed, it was because the Jews had poisoned the wells ; if a Christian child were lost, it had been crucified at a Jewish ceremony ; if a church sacristan was careless, it was the Jews who had stolen the Host from the altar to stab it with knives at the time of the Passover. In many periods, in almost all lands, whoever sinned or suffered, the Jew was accused, and the occasion straightway made use of for attacks in which hundreds or thousands might perish. The wild cry of the rabble, '*Hep! hep!*'—probably derived from the Latin formula, '*Hierosolyma est perdita*'—might break out at any time." [1]

E. The Jews in France.

The first monstrous blood accusation was raised against the Jews in France. In Blois (during

[1] Hosmer, *The Jews*.

the eleventh century) a mounted servant professed to have witnessed a Jewish rider throw the dead body of a child into the water. Count Theobald at once imprisoned all the Jews of the city. As the servant was the only witness, his truth was put to the test by his crossing the River Loire in a boat filled with water, and as he did this successfully it was regarded as proof of the guilt of the Jews, who were *condemned to death by fire*. They were secured in a wooden tower surrounded with fagots ; when this was done they were exhorted by a priest to save their lives by submitting to baptism, but in vain. Thirty-four men and seventeen women suffered death by fire, repeating Hebrew prayers.

" From these times there has been handed down a tragic Hebrew lay which affords a glimpse into the souls of those who thus suffered. It describes the immolation upon the funeral pile of a Rabbi and his family—a chant characteristically Jewish, pathetic, tenderly affectionate, but bitterly scornful to the last, and audacious in its imprecations. A few passages from this follow :

" ' Israel is in mourning, bewailing its brave martyred saints. Thou, O God, dost behold our flowing tears. Without Thy help we perish ! '

" ' O Sage, who day and night grew pale over the Torah, for the Torah you have died.'

" ' When his noble wife saw the flames burst forth : " My love calls me," she cried. " As he died, I would die." His youngest child trembled and wept. " Courage ! " said the elder. " In this hour Paradise will open." And the Rabbi's

JEWS MERE CHATTELS

daughter, the gentle maid? " Abjure your creed," they cry. " A faithful knight stands here who dies for love of thee." " Death by fire rather than renounce my God! it is God whom I desire for my spouse." " Choose," said the priest, " the cross or the torture." But the Rabbi said: " Priest, I owe my body to God, who now requires it," and tranquilly he mounts the pile.

" ' Together in the midst of the unchained flames, like cheerful friends at a festival, they raise high and clear the hymn of deliverance, and their feet would move in dances were they not bound in fetters.

" ' " God of vengeance, chastise the impious!"

" ' " Doth Thy wrath sleep?"

" ' " What are the crimes which I am forced to expiate under the torch of these felons?"

" ' " Answer, O Lord, for long have we suffered; answer, for we count the hours!"'"[1]

Philip IV. bought a Jew for 500 francs from the Count of Chablis, and another Jew with his children from his brother, Charles of Anjou.

On the accession of Philip Augustus, terrible times commenced for the Jews. He intended to overthrow the power of the barons and to make the throne supreme, and meant to attain his end by means of Jewish gold. In January, 1180, he caused all the Jews in his kingdom to be thrown into prison, and only let them free again on the payment of 15,000 marks in silver. The next year he banished all the Jews, confiscating all their landed property to the Crown. Later he

[1] Reinach, *Histoire des Juifs*.

favoured their return; but between the nobles and the King they led a miserable life, being sold like chattels with the estates of the nobles on which they lived, and were continually exposed to cruelty and robbery.

Philip IV. (1306) commanded all the Jews to leave the kingdom *within a month*, with loss of all their property and debts due to them, *on pain of death*. About 100,000 left the land with only the clothes they wore, and means of provision for one day. The King himself appropriated all their gold, money, jewels, and treasure in silver. The synagogue at Orleans was sold for 340 livres; that in Paris he presented to his coachman. Nine years later Louis X. permitted the return of the banished people.

In 1320 the shepherd scourge took place, marching with banners flying from town to town, like crusaders, joined as they went by highwaymen and other criminals. They attacked and destroyed the Jews, spoiling their property from the Garonne to Toulouse. Five hundred Jews perished in the fortified city of Verdun, and massacres of Jews occurred in the neighbourhood of Gascoigne, Bordeaux, Toulouse, and Albi; 120 Jewish communities were wiped out by them in the South of France.

In 1321 a number of ill-used lepers revenged themselves by poisoning springs and rivers, accusing the Jews of having incited them to do it, and of giving them the poison. In consequence, *Jews were again imprisoned, tortured, and done to death by fire.* In Chinon a great pit was dug, and eight Jews and Jewesses burnt in it. All Jews in France were condemned to pay the sum of £15,000. How the sponge was wrung dry from time to time, and why the poor people were permitted to return after spells of banishment it is easy to see.

Two centuries later the Jews were again accused of poisoning the wells and causing the plague, which in reality had travelled Westward from China. Under torture, by order of the Duke of Savoy, two Jews and a Jewess were forced to declare that the charge was true. *All the Jews* on the shores of the Lake of Geneva *were burnt alive*. The news was sent to Berne, where the Jews were again tortured and burnt; it passed to Basle, Strasbourg, Freiburg, Cologne, to Zurich, St. Gall, Schaffhausen, and many other cities; Jewish martyr fires lit up Southern France, Switzerland, and Germany.

A little later, when the French King John became a prisoner in England, and France, greatly impoverished, was unable to raise a ransom, the Jews saw their opportunity, and proposed to the Dauphin a plan by which the exiled Frenchmen, and Jews also, might settle in France under conditions alike favourable to the State and to themselves. The King agreed to this, and granted great privileges to the Jews, and liberty to settle in the land for twenty years. A year later he made certain modifications in the privilege granted, and eight years later his son, Charles V., issued a decree of banishment, which was but to squeeze the sponge a second time after a lapse of only nine years; for on the payment of 15,000 marks he recalled the edict of banishment. In 1394 hatred of the Jews had grown to such an extent that they were again banished by Charles VI. And four hundred years passed before their return; since which time they have for the most part escaped persecution, though the bitter spirit of animosity still exists, as was apparent not many years ago in the trial and unjust sentence of Captain Alfred Dreyfus, imprisoned in the barren rock prison of the Ile du Diable.

F. The Jews in England.

Even in dear old England, where in more recent times a limited number of Jews have found a home and have attained to a position of importance and prosperity, how terrible was their lot in the Dark Ages!

When exactly the Jews first found their way to Britain cannot be positively stated. It is certain that they were in these islands before the Norman Conquest; and already in the eighth century we read of repressive laws which were promulgated against them. Hatred of them broke out into a terrible flame at the coronation of Richard Cœur de Lion. " As Richard was returning to his palace from the coronation in the church, there entered into the state-room, among others who came to do homage to the King, a deputation of the richest and most prominent members of the whole Jewish community of England, to hand in their presents. On their appear-

CORONATION MASSACRE

ance, Baldwin, Archbishop of Canterbury, a fanatical Church dignitary, remarked darkly that no presents might be accepted from the Jews ; and that they must be dismissed from the palace, as through their religion they had forfeited the privilege to rank among other nations. Richard, who did not think to what evil consequences the expulsion of Jews would give occasion, innocently followed the instruction of the Archbishop. The palace menials, who showed the Jews out of the palace, thought to gain the approval of their masters by abusing them. The gaping crowd likewise fell to, and pursued the Jewish deputies with blows of the fist, with stones and clubs. Soon there spread about in all parts of London the false report that the King desired to humble and massacre the Jews, and immediately the mob and the crusading rabble trooped together to enrich themselves with the possessions of the Jews. The pillagers made an attack upon the houses in which the Jews had fortified themselves, and set fire to them. Meanwhile night had come, and covered with her shadows the ghastly butchery of the Jews. It was in vain that the newly-crowned King sent one of his courtiers, Ranulph de Granville, to make inquiries about the uproar, and put a stop to it. At first he could not make himself heard, and was moreover, assailed with jeers by the raging mob. Thus many Jews perished ; others killed themselves rather than submit to baptism. Most of the Jewish houses were burnt, and the synagogues destroyed." [1]

[1] Graetz, *History of the Jews.*

Richard did his best to put an end to the excesses committed at the time of his coronation by punishing the ringleaders ; but on his leaving England on the Third Crusade (1190) the massacres again began, Stamford, Lincoln, and Norwich being scenes of the worst examples of this mania for blood and plunder. In York the Jews fled for refuge to the Castle, defended themselves for a while under the lead of two brave men, and then by sword and fire took their own lives rather than submit to be baptized. Rich old Joceus, an inhabitant of York, who had suffered severely at the time of the Coronation massacre, was the first to kill his wife, and to fall by the hand of the Rabbi ; of a community of nearly 500 not one remained alive.

All Jews, with their property, were owned by the King, who had an exact inventory of the Jews, and their means, taken throughout his kingdom in order to know how much they were worth to him in realisable wealth. A Court of Exchequer of the Jews exercised control over all Jewish matters, with which in this land the Church had no voice at all ; but this was in order that the King himself should have complete cognisance of all their means and the opportunities by which he could express them to his own ends. No Jew could leave the land without permission of the Court of Exchequer of the Jews ; incredible sums were reaped by the King's purse for such permission. For the confirmation of a decree of Henry, John Lackland extorted the sum of 4,000 marks ; again in 1210 he obtained 60,000 marks. A Jew of Bristol was

BANISHMENT FROM ENGLAND 45

tortured by the cruel extraction of tooth after tooth, until the miserable man paid down the sum of 10,000 marks in silver. Under the regency of Stephen Langton, Archbishop of Canterbury, Jews were compelled to pay tithes to support the Church, and to wear the prescribed badge of shame ; they were forbidden to build synagogues, or to protect their property when spoliation was threatened by depositing it in the churches. Henry III. and Edward I. in a period of nine years extorted the sum of 8,400,000 marks (£420,000) from them ; Henry III. in person forcing from Aaron of York the sum of four gold marks and 4,000 silver marks. Edward I. forbade the Jews to be usurers ; and since this was the only means of livelihood left them, their case was evil indeed, and their Rabbis implored permission for them to quit the land. Blood accusations were trumped up against them, and in Easter week, 1264, some hundreds of Jews were massacred. In 1278 the Jews were accused of falsifying the coins ; all the Jews were imprisoned on one day and their houses searched ; *two hundred and ninety-three Jews were hung* on this occasion. Next year a blood accusation occurred in Northampton, and some Jews in London were first hanged and then quartered. And thus the record of oppression and suffering continues till 1290, when Edward I. issued his final Act of banishment against them.

On October 9th of that year the remnant of 16,000 Jews left the British shores, where they had lived for many generations, to begin a wandering life in other, not more hospitable, lands ; and from that day till the time of Cromwell (about three hundred and seventy years) the English law, and fear, prevented a single Jew from landing on these shores.

G. The Fiery Furnace in Germany.

When the Jews first settled in Germany is as little known as when they first came to France or England. Their first settlement in this part of Europe was probably Worms. One Jewish legend asserts that the Jews in the Rhine countries had lived there from the time of the Judges; and another legend in proof of the antiquity of the Jewish settlements in Germany avers that they were there already in the time of Ezra, who is alleged to have sent letters to them, admonishing them to come up to Jerusalem for the great feasts, but that they replied that in Worms on the Rhine they had found a new Jerusalem, and desired to know nothing of the old. But these are only legends invented in the Middle Ages in the hope of clearing themselves from the charge of having had any share in the crucifixion of Christ, and of escaping the frightful persecutions which so often threatened them, on the charge that their fathers had been the " murderers of God." It is only in the fourth century after Christ that any evidence exists of Jews dwelling in Cologne. When Charlemagne (797) sent an embassy to Harun al Raschid, the Jew Judah Isaac accompanied as interpreter. After the embassy had perished on the journey, the reply of the Sultan, with his presents, was brought back

HORRORS OF THE CRUSADES 47

by Isaac alone. In a solemn audience at Aix-la-Chapelle he gave them over to the Emperor.

The martyrology of the Jews in Germany begins with the first Crusade. The first two hordes (for they can scarcely be called armies), led by Peter the Hermit and the monk Gotschalk, left the Jews alone ; but behind these followed an immense rabble, made up of different nationalities, some two hundred thousand strong, including a host of bad women and girls, preceded by a goose and a goat. "In this vile horde no pretence was kept up of order or of decency. Sinning freely, it would seem, that grace might abound, they plundered and harried the lands through which they marched ; while three thousand horsemen, headed by some counts and gentlemen, were not too dignified to act as their attendants and to share their spoil."[1]

Words cannot describe the sufferings and agonies inflicted on the Jewish people by this lawless host as it swept across Europe. The course of blood was worst in Germany. A monk inflamed the fury of the rabble by showing them an inscription supposed to be found on the tomb of our Lord, to the effect that it was the duty of the faithful to *compel* the Jews first to embrace Christianity. Death or baptism ! *La mort ou le baptême!* they cried with the sword held to the breast of their victims.

As they approached Trier such terror fell on the Jews that some of them killed their own children ; matrons and maidens threw themselves into the Moselle, to perish in its waters, rather than

[1] *The Crusades*, by Rev. Sir G. W. Cox, Bart., M.A., p. 39.

live to meet the fate preparing for them. Mothers took their infants, and, loading themselves with stones, sprang with them from the bridge to certain death. Bishop Egilbert, appealed to by the Jewish community for protection, gave them the same alternative—baptism or death. At Spires the fanatics arrived on the Sabbath Day; they caught ten Jews and dragged them to the church to force them to be baptized, but they resisted, and all fell martyrs. Bishop John received and protected the Jewish community in his palace, for which kindness he is blamed in the Chronicles of Berthold von Constance.

At Worms the Bishop sheltered as many families as he was able; the rest made such defence as they could, but were overmastered and slain, women killing themselves and their children for dread of what would come upon them. Later the Bishop explained himself powerless to protect those who were yet in his palace unless they submitted to baptism. A short space was permitted them to decide. When the doors were at last forced open, a ghastly sight appeared, all the Jews lay dead in their own blood. The mob in revenge sought for any of their victims that might yet be in the city, and put them to cruel deaths. The Jewish community in Worms to this day observes a yearly fast in remembrance of the "saints"—some eight hundred—who perished in this massacre.

The history of the same time in Mainz and Cologne, Mörs, and the cities of the Rhine, is a story of blood and horror which passes

SELF-IMMOLATION

imagination or description. The despair which seized the Jews was such that in Cologne Samuel ben Jechiel, an aged Jew, took his young son, and after pronouncing a blessing over him, gave him his death blow, the boy acquiescing with his dying breath with an "Amen" to the deed. The old man then handed the knife to another Jew to be slain himself, the bystanders repeating aloud the Jewish confession of faith: "Hear, O Israel, the Lord thy God is one God," as was their custom in all times of massacre. After so doing they also perished, throwing themselves into the river. In another place the Jews chose five of their number to kill all the rest, and lastly themselves; the last man ended his life by precipitating himself from a high tower. What must not have been the terrors which faced the unhappy people throughout an entire continent at the hands of the *Christians* of their day, when they took such means to escape their fury!

Similar scenes were enacted in the second crusade, just fifty years later (1146). Pope Eugenius III. issued a Bull proclaiming that all who joined in the Holy War would be released from the interest which they owed to the Jews; while Peter, the Venerable Abbot of Clugny, exerted his influence to inflame Louis VII. of France, and other noble crusaders, against them. But "the appetite for blood among the hordes of the second crusade was whetted by the wolfish howlings of the monk Rudolph"[1] who travelled about everywhere preaching with tears in his eyes

[1] *The Crusades*, by Rev. Sir G. W. Cox, Bart., M.A., p. 88.

that all Jews should be slain as "murderers of our dear Lord." The worst fate again befell the Jews in Germany. "Even the partial protection which the citizens of the Rhineland had afforded the persecuted people in the First Crusade was now withdrawn, and the undisciplined mob gave the reins to the gratification of its religious zeal and of its lust."[1] It was then that Bernard of Clairvaux lifted up his voice on behalf of the Jews in his two famous epistles, one addressed to the Archbishop of Mayence and the other to the clergy and people of France and Bavaria. "The Jews," he says in the first, "ought not to be persecuted; they ought not to be slain; they ought not to be driven into banishment. Consult Holy Scripture. . . . These men are living monuments to remind us of the passion of Christ. For this cause they are dispersed in all countries, that while they suffer the just punishment of their heinous sins, they may be witnesses of our redemption . . . yet in the eveningtide of the world they will be converted, and He will remember them."[2] It was then also that the German Emperor took them under his protection; "but this favour was to cost the recipients dearly. Henceforth the German Jews were regarded as the Emperor's protégés, which gradually came to mean the Emperor's serfs. All they possessed, including their families and their own persons, were the Emperor's chattels, to be bought, sold, or pledged by him at pleasure.

[1] Abbott, *Israel in Europe*.
[2] The letters are given in full in *Israel and the Gentiles*, by Da Costa.

THE "JEW-SLAYERS"

They were designated 'chamber-servants' (*Servi Cameræ*, or *Kammerknechte*); a servitude, however, that had the advantage of making it the Emperor's interest to safeguard them against oppression, and to suffer no one to fleece them but himself." But even the power of the Emperor could not always shield them. Thus, to single out only a few out of numberless Jewish tragedies: in 1298 some hundred Jewish communities in Germany and Austria were destroyed by an infuriated Christian rabble, under the leadership of a fanatical noble named Rindfleisch, on the pretext that the Jews had stolen and desecrated the Host. "It had actually been seen that as they were pounding the wafer in a mortar, blood spurted up from it"! Once again we read of many Jewish mothers throwing their children into the flames and then destroying themselves rather than fall into the hands of the demon-possessed mobs.

In 1336—39, in the reign of the Emperor Louis of Bavaria, a similar scourge fell upon the Jews. A horde of peasants calling themselves "Jew-slayers," under the leadership of two nobles, swept through Alsace and the Rhinelands, plundering and murdering; one of the leaders (Armleder) declaring that he was commissioned by God to avenge "Christ's blood and wounds" on the Jewish people. But the sufferings of the Jews in Germany, "a chapter ages long," culminated at the time of the Black Death, 1348—50. "This scourge, which carried off a quarter of the population of Europe, afflicted the Jews but lightly on account of their isolation and their simple and wholesome way of life. This comparative exemption from the pest was enough to make them suspected. 'The Jews poison the wells and the springs,' it was said. The Rabbis of Toledo were believed to have formed a plot to destroy all Christendom. The composition of the poison, the colour of the packages in which it was transported, the emissaries who conveyed them, were all declared to have been discovered. Confirmations of these reports, extracted by torture from certain poor creatures, were forthcoming, and the people flew upon the Jews until entire communities were destroyed.

"The 'Flagellants,' fanatical sectaries, half naked and scourging themselves, swarmed through Germany preaching extermination to all unbelievers. Basle expelled its Jews, Freiburg burned them, Spires drowned them. The entire community at Strasbourg—two thousand souls—was dragged upon an immense scaffold, which was set on fire. At Worms, Frankfort, and Mainz, the Israelites anticipated their fate, setting their homes on fire and throwing themselves into the flames." [1]

H. The Jewish Tragedy in Spain and Portugal.

I fear the hearts of my readers are already quite sick with the details of the Jewish tragedy in different lands, as is that of the writer in compiling them. Yet to finish this imperfect summary of Jewish suffering in the Middle Ages I must

[1] Hosmer, *The Jews*.

THE GREEN BOOK OF ARAGON 53

add a brief outline of their history in one or two other Christian countries.

For some centuries the Jews suffered least of all in Spain, where some of them are supposed to have resided before the destruction of the second Temple, and where they took deep root and became very wealthy and powerful. Numbers embraced Christianity, and intermarried so largely with the noble families of the land, that it was said that in Aragon there was only one noble family which was not of partly Jewish extraction. "The Green Book of Aragon," written by Juan de Andreas, secretary of the Inquisition, in 1507, is a genealogy of baptized Jewish families, and confirms this statement. In the reign of Alfonso XI., 1325—50, their condition was so favourable that they imagined it could no longer be held true that the sceptre had departed from Judah, for the lordship and government of Spain was in their hands.

During the same reign, however, hatred against the Jews had already grown to an alarming extent. In 1348 the Black Death, to which reference has already been made more than once, travelled from far-off China, across Asia and Europe, sweeping about one-third of humanity from off the face of the earth. The Jews of Spain were accused of concocting a diabolical plan to destroy all the Christians in the world by poisoning all springs and wells. The Rabbis of Toledo in particular were named as the fiends who devised this plan of ridding themselves of their Christian oppressors at one stroke. "They had despatched messengers far and wide with boxes containing poison, and

54 A SUMMARY OF JEWISH HISTORY

with threats of excommunication had instigated all the Jews to aid in carrying out their plans. These directions to the Jews had issued from Toledo, which place was to all appearance the Jewish capital.

"The deluded and infatuated people even went so far as to point out by name the man who had delivered these orders and the poison. It was Jacob Pascate, said they, a man who had come from Toledo, and had settled in Chambery (in Savoy) : he it was who had sent out a whole troop of Jewish poisoners into all the different countries and cities. This Jacob, together with a Rabbi Peyret, of Chambery, and a rich Jew, Aboget, were said to have dealt largely in the manufacture and sale of poisons. The poison, which was prepared by the Jewish doctors of the Black Art in Spain, was sometimes reported to be concocted from the skin of a basilisk, or compounded of spiders, frogs, and lizards, or again from the hearts of Christians and the fragments of the Host, beaten into a soft mass. These and similar silly stories, invented by ignorant or perhaps malicious people, and distorted and exaggerated by the heated imagination, were credited not alone by the ignorant mob, but even by men of higher culture." [1]

Great excesses were committed against the Jews in different cities of the Peninsula, many of them being killed and their property plundered ; a wholesale massacre of all the Jews in the kingdom being averted only by a Papal Bull of Clement VI. (one

[1] Graetz, *History of the Jews*, vol. iv. p. 109.

FRAY VINCENTE FERRER

of the very few Popes who lifted up his voice in defence of the Jews) and by the intervention of the nobility. From this time onward, however, with short respites and brief intervals of prosperity, Israel's night of sorrow in Spain commenced.

One specially tragic chapter in the history of the Jews in Spain is that of the Marranos. In 1391, stirred up by the fiery eloquence of the fanatical priest Fernando Martinez, a series of wholesale massacres took place in Castile and Aragon. It commenced in Seville, where of the large and wealthy Jewish community about half were slain, and the other half to save their lives allowed themselves to be baptized. Of their three beautiful synagogues, two were turned into churches. The rising against the Jews spread itself all over Spain. Many thousands were sacrificed to priestly and popular rage, " and the cities of Toledo, Cordova, Catalonia, Barcelona, Valencia, as well as the island of Majorca, were coloured red with Jewish blood." Great numbers, however—according to von Döllinger two hundred thousand—submitted to baptism to save their lives. To these " converts " large numbers more were added by the unenlightened frenzied zeal of the Dominican monk Fray Vincente Ferrer, afterwards canonised by the Romish Church for his great services on her behalf.; a real ascetic, burdened by the corruptions of Christendom, and impelled by the belief that the end of the world and the Great Judgment were at hand, he went about preaching repentance in the monkish style, but with fiery zeal, and depicting in the most realistic

56 A SUMMARY OF JEWISH HISTORY

style the Passion of our Saviour. Weeping and lamentation broke forth among the audience wherever he preached. Encouraged by his success in the churches, he thought himself called to undertake the work of converting the Jews and Saracens; and for this purpose obtained not only a royal mandate to preach in the synagogues, but that the Jews should be *forced* to attend his sermons.

This "sincere but forbidding saint, who called his bigotry religion, and his hatred of heretics love to God," rushed from synagogue to synagogue, the crucifix in one hand, the Torah roll in the other, attended by a crowd of "Flagellants" and a bodyguard of lancers, preaching the Gospel of peace in a voice of thunder. "Impressive processions and sacred hymns, banners, crucifixes, and assaults on the Jewish quarter" by the Christian mob, had their desired effect, and large numbers of the confused and terrified Jews flocked to the churches to be baptized.

Now, there were some sincere converts to Christ among the Jews in Spain, several of them eminent for their learning and devotion to His cause (as there were, thank God ! in all other countries, and at all times—even in the darkest days of the Church's history), who must not be confounded, as Jewish historians maliciously attempt to do, with those who have been driven into the Church by fear, or who have themselves entered it out of indifference, or for worldly advantage. But the methods of the Dominicans and of the Romish Church generally were not only foreign to the spirit of the Gospel, but have resulted in incalcul-

THE MARRANOS

able injury to the cause of Christ; for these are largely responsible for the deep-seated hatred of the Jews to Christianity, and their prejudice against those who attempt to make the Gospel of their Messiah known among them.

These *Anusim* (forced converts), as the Jews called them, or *Marranos* ("the Damned") as the Spaniards called them, became eventually a curse to Spain, to their own people as well as to themselves. Many of them felt in their hearts a more intense antipathy to Christianity than when they had been openly opposed to it, but were obliged to live a lie. Outwardly they had to conform to the Church-regulated life of a Spaniard, while in secret they observed the Jewish rites and ceremonies. The new Christians soon began to be suspected by the old; moreover, the spirit of envy and jealousy took possession of multitudes of Spaniards, for these Marranos, by their wealth and intelligence, pressed themselves into all circles, and monopolised many important positions, not only in the State, but also in the Church. They intermarried with the highest in the land, many an impecunious noble seeking to make good his declining fortune by courting a fair daughter of "converted Israel."

But neither ecclesiastical nor civic honours nor social advancement could bring these *Marranos* to have faith in Christ, or into real sympathy with the Romish Church. Cardinal Mendoza, the Archbishop of Seville, was commanded by the Spanish sovereigns, "as a last resort before proceeding to extremes to set forth the doctrines of the

Catholic faith in a short catechism, and to cause his clergy to diffuse the light among the benighted Marranos "; but this also proved of no effect. " Such was the frame of the public mind when short-sighted statecraft, in the person of Ferdinand, King of Aragon, was wedded to narrow piety in that of Isabella, heiress to the crown of Castile. The legitimate offspring of such a union could be no other than persecution. But even if the sovereigns had been enlightened and tolerant, it is doubtful whether they could have stemmed the current.

" In 1473 the mob massacred the Constable of Castile at Jaen, because he attempted to repress its fury ; and after Isabella the Catholic's accession to the throne, petitions poured in from all sides, clamouring for the extirpation of the 'Jewish heresy.' The bigots of Seville, headed by the Dominican Prior of the monastery of St. Paul, agitated for the introduction of the Inquisition. Their demand was seconded by the Papal Nuncio ";[1] but only after seven years (on September 17, 1480) did Ferdinand and Isabella at last yield to the popular clamour.

The Inquisition—the very mention of which sends a shudder through our whole being, and which afterwards directed its devilish machinery also against the saints of God who broke away from the superstitions of Rome—was thus established in the first instance to terrify into faithfulness apostate Jews, the sincerity of whose conversion to Christianity was suspected, and in

[1] Abbott, *Israel in Europe*.

THE INQUISITION

almost all cases with good reason. " Seated in some vast and frowning castle, or in some sunless cavern of the earth, its ministers chosen from the most influential men of the nation, its familiars in every disguise, in every corner of the land, its proceedings utterly secret, its decrees over-riding every law, it would be impossible to draw a picture which would exaggerate its accumulated horrors. Men and women disappeared by hundreds, suddenly and completely as a breath annihilates the flame of a lamp, some gone for ever, without a whisper as to their fate ; some to reappear in after years, halt through long tortures, pale and insane through frightful incarceration. When, in the cities the frequent processions wound through the streets, with their long files of victims on the way to the place of burning, children, bereaved of father and mother, flocked to see whether among the doomed they might not catch a last look at the face of the long lost parent. The forms that were observed were such a mockery of justice ! In the midst of the torture came the cold interrogation of the inquisitor. Fainting with terror and anguish, the sufferer uttered he knew not what, to be written down by waiting clerks and made the basis of procedure. Grace Aquilar, in one of her stories, makes her heroine to disappear through the floor of a chamber of Queen Isabella herself, who had sought to protect her ; borne then by secret passages to a vast hall, where a grandee of Spain superintends cruelties of which my words give but an adumbration. She recites the traditions that have come down in Jewish families, and history confirms all that they report. No earthly power could save, no human fancy can paint the scene too dark."

The Inquisition had not been in existence three days when six wretched Marranos suffered at the stake ; and the Jesuit historian Mariana informs us that the net total of victims for the first year amounted to 2,000 burnt alive and 17,000 sentenced to loss of property, loss of civil rights, or incarceration. Already in the following year the first *auto-da-fé* took place ; and to give my readers an idea of what this meant, I include a description from a Jewish writer of one celebrated just two hundred years later (in 1680) in honour of the marriage of Charles II. with Marie Louise, niece of Louis XIV. :

"Upon the great square in Madrid an amphitheatre was reared, with a box for the Royal Family upon one side, opposite to which was a daïs for the grand inquisitor and his train. The Court officials were present in gala uniforms, the trade guilds in their state dresses, the orders of monks, and an immense concourse of the populace. From the church towers pealed the bells, among whose sounds were heard the chants of the monks. At eight o'clock entered the procession. Before the grand inquisitor was borne the green cross of the Holy Office, while the bystanders shouted, 'Long live the Catholic faith!' First marched a hundred charcoal-burners, dressed in black and armed with pikes. It was their prescriptive right to lead the procession, as having furnished the

AN AUTO-DA-FE

fuel for the sacrifice. A troop of Dominican monks followed, then a duke of the bluest blood, hereditary standard-bearer of the Holy Office. After friars and nobles, carrying banners and crosses, came thirty-five effigies of life size, with names attached, borne by familiars of the Inquisition, representing condemned men who had died in prison or escaped. Other Dominicans appeared, a ghastly row, carrying coffins containing the bones of those convicted of heresy after death; then fifty-four penitents, with the dress and badge of victims, bearing lighted tapers. In turn came a company of Jews and Jewesses (in the interval since Ferdinand and Isabella a few wretched Jews had ventured back into Spain), mostly persons of humble rank, in whom the interest of the ceremony chiefly centred; these were to be burned as obstinate in their refusal of the faith. Each wore a cloak of coarse serge, yellow in colour, covered with representations, in crimson, of flames, demons, serpents, and crosses. Upon their heads were high pointed caps, with placards in front bearing the name and offence of the wearer. Haggard they were through long endurance of dungeon damp and darkness, broken and torn from the torture chambers, glad, for the most part, that the end of their weary days had come.

"As the procession moved past the station of the royal personages, a girl of seventeen, whose great beauty had not been destroyed, cried out aloud from among the condemned to the young queen: 'Noble queen, cannot your royal presence save me from this? I sucked in my religion with my mother's milk ; must I now die for it ? ' The queen's eyes filled with tears, and she turned away her face. She was unused to such sights. Even she, probably, could not have interceded without danger to herself. The supplicating girl passed on with her companions to her fate. High Mass having been performed, the preliminaries to the terrible concluding scene are transacted. The sun descends, the Angelus is rung from the belfries, the vespers are chanted, the multitude proceeds to the place of suffering. It is a square platform of stone in the outskirts of the city, at whose four corners stand mis-shapen statues of the prophets. Those who repent at the last moment have the privilege of being strangled before burning. The effigies and bones of the dead are first given to the flames. Last perish the living victims, the king himself lighting the fagots ; their constancy is so marked that they are believed to be sustained by the devil. Night deepens ; the glare of the flames falls upon the cowl of the Capuchin, the cord of the Franciscan—upon corselet and plume—everywhere upon faces fierce with fanaticism. In the background rises the gloomy city—all alight as if with the lurid fire of hell ! ''.

Leaving the Marranos and turning again to the general history of the Jews in Spain, the final and greatest calamity that befell them in that land has yet to be told.

On March 31, 1492, the decree was finally signed by Ferdinand and Isabella in the magnificent Alhambra of Granada (about three months after the final overthrow of the Moors and their triumphal entry into that city) that all the Jews of Spain, Sicily, and Sardinia must quit those countries within four months on pain of death; the reason adduced in the edict being that they were the occasion of, and abetted, the relapses into Judaism on the part of the " New Christians," or Marranos. They might take their property with them, with the exception of gold, silver, coins, or such articles as were forbidden to be exported; but as by far the greater part of their wealth consisted in these very precious metals and money, it practically implied also the confiscation of their property.

It is related that when the decree of expulsion of the Jews was promulgated, Abrabanel, a Jew himself and Lord of the Treasury, with the most eminent Marranos of the Palace, came to the Catholic sovereigns with the offer of a large sum of money to induce them to recall the decree; but that when Torquemada, the Grand Inquisitor, learned this, he hastened to the palace, and holding the crucifix before Ferdinand and Isabella said: " Judas sold Christ for thirty pieces of silver; your majesties are willing to do so for thirty thousand. Here He is; take and sell Him." This had the desired effect, and the doom of the Jews in Spain was sealed.

For the finest palaces and houses the poor exiles obtained a mere song. Why should the Christians buy when they knew that the Jews would have to leave all behind anyhow? A piece of cloth was offered for a vineyard, an ass for a house. The

64 A SUMMARY OF JEWISH HISTORY

Inquisition even forbade Christians to sell them any food.

On August 2, 1492, which happened to fall on the 9th of Ab—the day of such sorrowful associations to the Jewish nation (on which both the first and second Temples were destroyed)—about 400,000 Jews left Spain, that " happy land," as they once used to call it ; the " accursed land," as it has since been known among them—to go forth they knew not whither.

To help them forget their sorrows, the Rabbis caused companies of trumpeters and pipers to head the mournful pilgrim procession. In Segovia the last three nights were spent in weeping and prayer by the graves of their fathers. The tale of their wanderings is most woeful. Misery and dire need, robbery, hunger, and the plague overtook them ; many were sold in foreign lands as slaves ; many were drowned, many burnt on ships at sea ; 12,000 who sought refuge in the neighbouring kingdom of Navarre had the usual conditions proposed to them—exile or baptism. Those who sought safety in Oran and Algiers were prevented landing on account of the plague which had broken out among them ; and when later they did land, they were not permitted to enter the towns. A fire broke out among their wooden huts and reduced them all to ashes. In Fez they were nowhere allowed inside the towns, and had to subsist, like the animals, on herbs. Fathers were obliged to sell their children as slaves that they might not die of hunger ; mothers killed themselves and their children ; sailors tempted children to the ships by offer of food in order to sell them as slaves. The Genoese seamen were worst of all in their treatment of the fugitives. They threw many into the sea, and it is related that, actuated by greed, they cut many of their victims open in search of jewels and coins which they might have swallowed in order to retain them. Those who were landed were permitted to remain in Genoa three days only, unless they would submit to baptism. The children were so hungry that they crept into the town and the churches, consenting to be baptized for a bit of bread. In Corfu and Candia they were sold into slavery, and were bought by Persians, who hoped to extract large sums from the Persian Jews for their release.

The Jews in Portugal.

The history of the Jews in Portugal is, to a large extent, linked with and very similar to that of their brethren in Spain. Here, too, they could look back to a golden age of prosperity, and there were times when the destiny of the kingdom might almost be said to have been in Jewish hands. But soon Israel's night of weeping commenced here too. Already, early in the fourteenth century, we read of anti-Jewish decrees and the imposition of the badge of shame. From time to time excesses were also committed against them by mobs urged on thereto by the preaching of the monks. Their sorrows in this kingdom, however, culminated shortly subsequent to the Spanish catastrophe in 1492. When the decree for their expulsion from the Peninsula was signed, many Spanish Jews desired to settle in Portugal; but with the exception of a limited number of artisans, armourers, and other workers in metal, permission was refused: the rest were only permitted on payment of twenty marks in gold each to remain eight months, after which the King promised to provide ships and a cheap passage to any land in which they might choose to settle. One hundred and twenty thousand came to Portugal on these conditions, in the hope, most probably, that the time limit would be lengthened or removed. Popular feeling, however, was against them; and as the plague made its appearance in Portugal soon after, the unfortunate Jews were accused of having brought it to the country, and the populace clamoured for their departure.

Ships were provided at the end of eight months to take them whither they would or could go; but the sailors extorted from them all they had, refused them food except at exorbitant prices, committed outrages on the women and girls, and finally landed the wretched people in desert parts on the African coast, where they were left to perish of hunger or to be carried as slaves by the Moors. Those who were in the country after the eight months, were declared by King Joao to be his slaves, whom he proceeded to present to the different grandees of his kingdom. To add to their anguish their children were torn from them and shipped to the island of St. Thomas, there to be forcibly baptized and brought up as Christians. So much for these poor Spanish exiles; there still remained in the kingdom the native Portuguese Jews, who had been in the country for centuries.

In 1495 King Manoel came to the throne. This prince was at first favourably inclined to his Jewish subjects; but, unfortunately for Portugal as well as for the Jews, he entered into negotiations for a marriage with the Infanta Isabella, a daughter of Ferdinand and Isabella of Spain, who had already been married to the Infante of Portugal, but soon after became a widow; the Spanish Court would listen to the proposal only on two conditions—firstly, that he should break off friendly relations with the Court of France, and, secondly, that he should banish all the Jews out of his kingdom. Both proposals were repugnant to Manoel; but after a time of hesitation, being deeply enamoured with the Infanta, he weakly yielded. This Isabella herself seemed to excel her own mother in bigotry. When King Manoel was at last expecting his bride to cross the borders of his country, he received a letter from her, saying that she would never set foot in Portugal until the land had been cleansed from the "curse-laden Jews."

The marriage contract had therefore to be sealed in the misery of the Jewish people. The King promulgated an edict that all the Jews of his kingdom must either be baptized or leave the country after a few months' respite on pain of death. Only a few, however, chose the alternative of baptism, which aggravated the King, who wanted very much to retain the Jews in his country. A decree was issued that all Jewish children under fourteen years must be baptized before or on Easter Sunday, 1497. The agony which this occasioned to the Jewish parents cannot be described. Some killed their own children, some threw them into rivers and wells to prevent what they feared for them even more than death. Many parents and children were torn from one another by the whip and scourge, and then dragged by the hair to the baptismal font, the poor children being afterwards distributed among Christians to be brought up as such.

Some of the Jews now asked for baptism merely in order to retain their children, but only afterwards, as suspected Marranos, to be followed by fire and sword by the Inquisition. At last Manoel appointed the single harbour of Lisbon as the place of departure for the remaining Jews of Portugal. Some twenty thousand of the wretched people assembled; but so many difficulties were put in their way that a large number were unable to leave by the appointed time, whereupon the King declared them to be his slaves. Later, again, he promised them honour and privileges if they would submit to baptism; and when this did not succeed, he kept them three days without bread and water. Again abominable scenes occurred, and aged men were dragged by their beards, or hair, or by ropes, to the churches, to be forcibly baptized; from which they saved themselves only by suicide, either without or within the churches. In the year 1500 two thousand " new Christians," or Jewish Marranos, were massacred in Lisbon within three days.

I. The Jews in Poland.

It would be a weary task to trace the story of the scattered people in fuller detail, or to follow their wanderings in lands not included in the above summary; but it is a striking fact that there is no country in which Jews are found in any appreciable numbers where their history—however bright and promising it may have been for a time—does not end in tragedy. A striking illustration of this is presented by the history of the Jews in Poland. Here, too, as in Spain and Portugal, they could look back to a golden age lasting several centuries, when, as the only middle class between the luxurious, easy-going magnates and the serfs, they were indispensable in the land, and became all-powerful. In the thirteenth, fourteenth, and fifteenth centuries, when such terrible calamities fell on their brethren in the more "advanced" southern countries of Europe, the Jews in Poland dwelt in peace and prosperity.

In the reign of Casimir the Great (1333—70), who seemed to have been much in the power of a Jewish favourite named Esther, who knew how to exercise her influence over the King for the advantage of her people, the Jews seemed to enjoy greater privileges in the land than the Christians. No wonder that it became a land of refuge for many thousands of the persecuted race from all other countries, and that the Jews of Poland and Lithuania became known throughout Europe not only for their worldly prosperity, but also for their Talmudic learning and cabalistic casuistry. But

70 A SUMMARY OF JEWISH HISTORY

here, too, the Jews could not escape the common fate of the Jewish people since the destruction of Jerusalem. "When the bow of Jewish prosperity was overstrained it snapped in two."[1] The occasion was as follows: The Cossacks, a people half-savage, composed of escaped Russian convicts, peasants, and adventurers, were permitted to settle on the frontier districts between Poland, Tartary, and Turkey in order that they might be a protection to Poland from attacks by Tartars and Turks. The government of the Cossack colonies, the courts of justice, taxes, the trade in spirit, and other products of the soil—in fact, everything that related to their settlements—was in the hands of Jewish agents, employed by the nobles who owned the land. Not even a baptism or wedding could take place without the Greek Pope obtaining the key of the church from a Jewish custodian. As the Jesuits grew in power in Poland they tried to force the Roman Catholic faith on the Cossacks, and in this they were abetted by the Jews, who hoped to further their own interests with the Polish King by this means. They procured instead only the intensified hatred of the Cossacks, which soon burst forth in a flame of terrible vengeance.

In the first Cossack rising of 1638, which was quickly suppressed, two hundred Jews perished. Confident that their Messiah would appear in the year 1648, and that all power would then be theirs, the Jews continued to abuse the power they possessed. Instead of the vain hope of the advent of the Messiah being realised, 1648 proved to be

[1] Heman, *Geschichte des Jüdischen Volkes.*

the commencement of terrible disasters to the Jews. All the Ukraine flamed into war. The Cossacks, under the leadership of the terrible Chmielnicki, joining with the Tartars, beat the Polish army, leading eight thousand Poles, with their prince, captives to Tartary. Then ensued a terrible time, the Cossack companies devastating the whole land as far as Kiev, murdering and spoiling all Jews. The perfidious Poles, not unfrequently, under promise of being spared themselves, gave up the Jews who had taken refuge in their strongholds to the power of their cruel foe ; six thousand Jews perished in this way in Nemirow. The Rabbi was spared only till he was made to disclose the hiding-place of the Jews' treasure, then he, too, fell a victim.

At Tulczin fifteen hundred Jews were done to death who would not receive baptism ; ten Rabbis were spared for the sake of the ransom which might be wrung from their communities. The Cossacks penetrated into Little Russia, annihilating all Jews. In Homel the Jews were driven naked into the fields, surrounded by the Cossacks, and fifteen hundred men, women, and children, who would not be baptized, were put to barbarous deaths. Thousands fled to Polonnoie, where they were treacherously given over to their foes. Hundreds and thousands of Jews perished in numerous other towns. Hunger and the plague made frightful ravages among the destitute Jewish fugitives. Throughout Podolia, Volhynia, and West Russia the Jews, the nobles, and the clergy shared the same terrible fate. On one occasion a hundred Jewish children were killed and thrown to the dogs. The Cossack leader extorted from the Jesuit prelate-king of Poland, as terms of peace, that Jews should be excluded from living, owning land, or farming, throughout the Ukraine, West Russia, Kiev, and a part of Podolia. In 1651 the war was renewed, and the advantage appeared to be with the Poles. The King now dictated a treaty of peace, with conditions, permitting the Jews their old rights of settlement in the Ukraine ; but this did not help them, and only led to fresh disaster. The Cossacks appealed for help to Russia, and now the unhappy Jews of Lithuania and West Poland, hitherto unmolested, had to endure unspeakable sufferings and almost wholesale slaughter. Among other places a terrible massacre took place in Wilna, the capital of Lithuania, and the large Jewish community there was almost annihilated. Then came the invasion of Poland by Charles X. of Sweden, which again brought terrible sufferings to the Jews. Poles, Russians, Cossacks, Swedes, Prussians, and Transylvanians ravaged the land, and the Jews always were especially the victims of their worst ferocity.

Thus the might and prosperity of the Jews in Poland came to an almost sudden and tragic end. Thousands wandered forth into other lands, and those that remained sunk into ever lower depths of poverty and wretchedness.

J. The Reformation and Since.

With the Reformation there commenced a new period of the world's history, and the principles

LUTHER AND THE JEWS

which were then promulgated could not but eventually affect the Jews also among those peoples by whom they were adopted. Yet it cannot be said that for a considerable period subsequent to that great movement their condition was very materially altered or their sufferings much lessened. Indeed, it is humiliating to find that some of the reformers, men of God though they were, had no more place in their hearts for compassion for this long oppressed people than their papal antagonists. Luther himself is a notable illustration of this. He began well. In his exposition of Psalm xxii. he blames the cruelty of the nations toward the Jews, and describes the enormities which have been committed against them as " worse than beastly."[1] In 1523 he published a remarkable book with the startling title *Dass Jesus ein Geborene Jude Gewesen* (*That Jesus was born a Jew*), in which he says, among other things: "Those fools the papists, bishops, sophists, monks, have formerly so dealt with the Jews, that every good Christian would rather have been a Jew. And if I had been a Jew, and seen such stupidity and such blockheads reign in the Christian Church, I would rather be a pig than a Christian. They have treated the Jews as if they were dogs, not men, and as if they were fit for nothing but to be reviled. They are blood relations of our Lord; therefore if we respect flesh and blood, the Jews belong to Christ more than we. I beg, therefore, my dear Papists, if you become tired of abusing me as a heretic, that you

[1] *Geschichte des Jüdischen Volkes*, p. 420.

begin to revile me as a Jew. Therefore it is my advice that we should treat them kindly ; but now we drive them by force, treating them deceitfully or ignominiously, saying they must have Christian blood to wash away the Jewish stain, and I know not what nonsense. Also we prohibit them from working amongst us, from living and having social intercourse with us, forcing them, if they would remain with us, to be usurers."

But Luther, who in some respects reminds one of the Apostle Paul, lacked not only the patience and Christlike spirit of the great Apostle, but the prophetic light and insight into God's plan and purpose with this unique people which would have enabled him to persevere in his love for them in spite of all their opposition and hardness of heart. Because they were not converted in masses, and stirred by their continued opposition to the Gospel and the sins of some individual Jews, he turned against them in great bitterness ; so much so that it seems scarcely credible that it could have been the same Luther, who in 1523 wrote *Dass Jesus ein Geborene Jude gewesen*, that twenty-one years later (in 1544) wrote *Von den Juden und Ihren Lügen* (*About the Jews and their Lies*), which breathes fire and sword against them, and in which he seeks to stir up the same spirit of hatred against them among the Protestant peoples and princes which he had previously denounced among the Catholics. If " the denunciations of Israel by the early Fathers of the Church had continued to dictate Christian intolerance through the ages, and their authority was quoted in support of the persecutions and massacres which sullied mediæval Europe, Luther's utterances exercised a similar influence over the Protestant world, both in his own and after times, down to the present day. Protestant Germany took up the tale of persecution in the sixteenth century where Catholic Germany had left off in the fifteenth. The Jews were given the alternative of baptism and banishment in Berlin, were expelled from Bavaria in 1553, from Brandenburg in 1573, and the tragedy of oppression was carried on through the ensuing centuries."[1]

Nor has Israel ceased to weep since their so-called " emancipation " ushered in late in the eighteenth century, when, chiefly through the influence of the French Revolution, civil and political rights have been granted to them in most of the countries in Europe, but not in those lands where the *great bulk* of the scattered people is to be found.

Indeed, the sorrows of Israel within these past ten years in the great Northern Empire of Russia (where more than half of the whole Jewish nation lives in a condition of more or less chronic wretchedness) and in Roumania, etc., have been such as to move even hard-hearted worldly men with compassion for them. " The picture," says Max Nordau in a masterly and comprehensive *Survey of the General Condition of the Jews at the Close of the Nineteenth Century* presented by him at the first Zionist Congress, " might almost be tinted as a monochrome, for wherever Jews are

[1] Abbott, *Israel in Europe*, p. 227.

dwelling in any number among the nations there Jewish misery prevails. This misery is not that of mere common poverty, which, according to the unchanging lot of earth, is ever our unfailing companion. It is a peculiar misery which befalls the Jews, not as men, but as Jews, and from which they would not suffer were they not Jews. Jewish distress is of two kinds, physical and moral.

"In Eastern Europe, in North Africa, in Western Asia, exactly in those lands where the overwhelming majority of Jews, probably ninetenths of them, dwell, Jewish misery is to be understood literally. It is a daily physical oppression, a terror of the day to follow, a tortuous struggle to support a bare existence. In Western Europe the battle of life is of late somewhat easier, although indications are not lacking to show that even here it may become more severe. But still, for the time being the question of food and shelter, of safety of body and life, is less anxious. Here the misery is of a moral description, and consists in daily mortification of self-respect and sense of honour, in the rough suppression of their effort to attain complete mental rest and satisfaction which none who is not a Jew need deny himself."

No wonder that in a very eloquent address on the same subject two years later he pathetically exclaimed: "We are living like Troglodytes, in perpetual darkness. To us the sun of justice is not shining. We are living like the creatures in the depths of the ocean. Upon us press the weight of a thousand atmospheres of mistrust and disdain. We have lived for centuries in a glacial period, surrounded by the bitter cold of malice and hatred. These are the permanent powers which have permanently influenced us, without noise, without incident to give rise to sensational reports, yet under which we have retrograded steadily, gradually, and unmistakably."

And not only are the great majority of the Jewish people full of sorrow and wretchedness from within, but they have been for many centuries, and still continue to be, a butt and a derision from without.

> "Thou makest us a strife unto our neighbours,
> And our enemies laugh unto themselves."

One need only be reminded of the ever present "Jewish Question" in all the lands of their dispersion, or have even a very slight acquaintance with the references to the Jews in the literature of the Middle Ages; one need only note the coarse jests and unjustifiable gibes, the shameful caricatures of the Jews to be found in the trashy anti-Semitic effusions of the "most civilised" nations of Europe at the present day; one need only be reminded of the fact that the honourable name of "Jew" has become a proverb and a byword among all the nations of the earth—to see how truly these words of the Psalmist have been and are still being fulfilled.

"What strikes one as very remarkable" observed von Döllinger, the President of the Academy of Sciences in Munich, in an address on "The Jews in Europe," delivered before that

78 A SUMMARY OF JEWISH HISTORY

learned body in 1881, "is that in the 'Christian' chronicles and histories of the Middle Ages no sign of compassion, not a word of indignation, is to be met with in their reports of the outrages committed against the Jews. *Many of the clerical chroniclers even manifest their pleasure in them.* Thus, for instance, the monk of Waverly relates in a triumphant tone the slaughter in London at the coronation of Richard I., which had taken place without any cause being given for it by the Jews, and concludes by exclaiming : " Blessed be the Lord who hath delivered up the wicked." [1] Truly Israel has had, and still has, much cause for weeping !

And it is a pathetic and sorrowful sight to see Israel weep. " Go to Jerusalem," wrote the late Franz Delitzsch in an early number of his *Saat auf Hoffnung*, " and there you can see it. On the south-western side of the Temple hill, where the tremendous ruins of the area of Solomon's Temple stand, is ' the Wailing Place of the Jews.' As their fathers of yore by the waters of Babylon, so the elders of the daughter of Zion mourn here every Friday, laying their hoary heads low in the dust by the crumbling Temple wall, and their tears fall in torrents on the open page of the Book of Lamentations, which they hold with their trembling hands. Youths, lying on their faces, moisten the penitential Psalms of David with their tears. Maidens, with dishevelled hair, bow their heads to the ground, kissing the ancient

[1] *Annals Monast.*, p. 246.

stones, and weeping for the misery of their people."

"Mournfully the Precentor begins the chant of lamentation :

"'Because of the palace that lies desolate.'

"And the people respond :

"'We sit solitary and weep.'

"The Precentor then continues his plaint :

"'Because of the temple that is destroyed,'
"'Because of the walls that are laid low,'
"'Because of our glory, that is departed from us,'
"'Because of the great men that are no more among us.'

"And again the people answer :

"'We sit solitary and weep.'

"Once more the Precentor continues :

"'Because of the precious stones that are burnt,'
"'Because of our priests that have stumbled,'
"'Because of our kings that have despised Him.'

"And ever more plaintive comes the response of the people :

"'We sit solitary and weep.'"

CHAPTER IV

THE PRIMARY CAUSE OF JEWISH SUFFERINGS; ISRAEL A PROPHET OF JUDGMENT

EVEN more sad and pathetic than actually to see Israel weep at the "Wailing Place," and in their synagogues on the 9th of Ab, and on other solemn occasions, is the thought that to this day they neither know nor acknowledge the real and underlying *cause* of all their sorrows and their sufferings.

This indeed constitutes the saddest symptom of Israel's present spiritual blindness. They have a zeal for their God, but not according to knowledge; they feel the Lord's hand heavy upon them, but they know not *wherefore;* they are smitten and even delude themselves into the belief that "they as a nation are the promised Messiah who are to atone for the sins of the world by unspeakable suffering." Their leaders and teachers blame the cruelty and inhumanity of the Gentile nations, and verily the nations of Christendom in particular have a terrible account yet to settle with God for their attitude and dealings with the Jewish

GOD'S ANGER

people ;[1] but behind these, for the most part apostate and corrupt nations who were used as God's scourge, there is *the anger of God.*

"O Jehovah, God of Hosts,
   How long wilt Thou be angry [lit. "smoke"] against the prayer of Thy people?" (ver. 4.)

The expression is a very striking one. Other scriptures speak of *God's anger* as "smoking," but here the figure is applied to Himself—" How long wilt *Thou* smoke?" Yes, alas! the Light of Israel, He who should have been their "Sun and Shield" has become a smoking furnace, and a

---

[1] We are sometimes asked, "But have not the sufferings of Israel all been minutely foretold by Moses and the prophets in advance?" Yes, certainly they have all been foretold; but have not the sufferings of Christ been even more minutely foretold and described also? And yet we read that it was "with wicked hands" that they took and crucified Him, and Israel was held responsible for their conduct and dealings in relation to Him. Prophecy, my dear reader, is given to us, not that it *may* be fulfilled, but because the omniscient God, who sees the end from the beginning, knows that it *shall* be fulfilled, and man is left a free and responsible agent; and the nations who know not that the great God is overruling all things, even their wicked actions, to the fulfilment of His predetermined counsel, are held accountable for their deeds.

And that the "jealousy" and hot displeasure of Jehovah against the nations because of their attitude to Israel are to be dreaded, history also testifies. Where are the great nations of antiquity who have lifted up their hands against the Jewish people? And in modern times the ancient word which He spoke to Abraham is still verifying itself in the experience of nations as of individuals: "I will bless them that bless thee, and him that curseth thee will I curse." (From the Author's *Notes on Zechariah.*)

consuming fire to His own people ; or in the words of the national song which God commanded Moses to write and to put into their mouth (Deut. xxxi. 14—23) that in case of their apostasy from Him it may be an everlasting witness against them :

"Because he forsook God which made him,
And lightly esteemed the God of his salvation,

*   *   *   *   *

Jehovah saw it, and abhorred them,
Because of the provocation of his sons and his daughters.
And He said, I will hide My face from them,
I will see what their end shall be :
For they are a very froward generation,
Children in whom is no faith.
They have moved Me to jealousy with that which is not God ;
They have provoked Me to anger with their vanities :
And I will move them to jealousy with those which are not a people ;
I will provoke them to anger with a foolish nation.
For a fire is kindled in Mine anger,
And burneth unto the lowest pit,
And devoureth the earth with her increase,
And setteth on fire the foundations of the mountains.
I will heap mischiefs upon them ;
I will spend Mine arrows upon them :
They shall be wasted with hunger, and devoured with burning heat
And bitter destruction ;
And the teeth of beasts will I send upon them,
With the poison of crawling things of the dust.
Without shall the sword bereave,
And in the chambers terror ;
It shall destroy both young man and virgin,
The suckling with the man of grey hairs."

(Deut. xxxii. 18–25.)

A UNIQUE PUNISHMENT

It is also a remarkable fact of history that the sufferings of the Jewish people since the destruction of the second Temple, which inaugurated the second stage of their dispersion among the nations, have been much more terrible than those which followed the destruction of the first Temple. Now we know the special great national sin of Israel which brought about the overthrow of the Northern Kingdom and the seventy years' captivity in Babylon; but what can be the outstanding great and awful sin of the Jewish nation which has been visited by God with a punishment so unique and unparalleled, and with a bondage lasting already nearly two thousand years? To this question neither the synagogue nor the Rabbis have any answer. Idolatry has been detested by the Jews ever since the captivity in Babylon. It is a matter of fact also that they have, as a people, outwardly at any rate, been more obedient to the letter of the Law—more " religious " and zealous for God at the time and since the appearing of Christ, than their fathers were before them. Not content merely with the Law, they have elaborated the Talmud, and have added innumerable precepts and commandments which have made Rabbinic Judaism a burden heavy indeed to be borne. To their superior morality and certain outstanding national virtues even their enemies have had to bear witness; for " in the vast mass of exhortatory sermons, accusations, and hostile declamations against the Jews, which in the endless representation of stereotyped phrases, pervades the ecclesiastical literature of the Middle Ages, their moral life, as far as regards family, chastity, temperance, faith in the performance of agreement, is never impeached." [1] Indeed, it is their tenacious adherence to their religion, and their zeal for their Law, which was one chief cause of the accusations and persecutions which have been heaped upon them. What, then, I repeat, can be the great sin which has caused God to hide His face from His chosen people for so long, and which has occasioned Israel's weary wanderings as a fugitive among the nations for so many centuries?

Alas! "Israel doth not know, My people doth not consider," nor will they acknowledge it as a nation until the spirit of grace and supplication shall be poured upon them, and they "*look upon Him whom they have pierced.*" Then with broken hearts they shall confess, like Joseph's brethren of old: "*We are verily guilty concerning our brother*" (Jesus, of whom Joseph is such a beautiful type)—" in that we saw the anguish of his soul, when he besought us, and we would not hear; *therefore* is this distress come upon us" (Gen. xlii. 21). Then Israel's greatest but *final* mourning will take place—*a weeping, not on account of their sufferings, but their great national sin.* "*They shall mourn for Him,* as one mourneth for his only son, and they shall be in bitterness for Him as one that is in bitterness for his firstborn. In that day shall there be a great mourning in Jerusalem ... and the whole land shall mourn, every family apart, and their wives apart" (Zech. xii. 10-14). Then, and only then, also shall Israel be finally comforted: then the "oil of joy shall

[1] Von Döllinger.

"A PROPHET OF JUDGMENT"

be given to them for mourning, the garment of praise for the spirit of heaviness." "And the ransomed of Jehovah shall return, and come to Zion with songs and everlasting joy upon their heads, they shall obtain joy and gladness, and sorrow and sighing shall flee away." (Isa. xxxv. 10 ; lxi. 3).

But till then, in the words of one of Israel's noblest and most gifted sons,[1] Israel has been, and must remain "*a prophet of judgment.*"

"'The Lord is righteous' is Israel's cry in Lam. i. 18, 'for I have rebelled against His commandment.' 'Now I know that the Lord is greater than all gods,' says Jethro, 'for in the thing wherein they dealt proudly He was above them ' (Exod. xviii. 11).

"Israel is a prophet of judgment. When he had taken prisoner the heathen king Adoni-bezek, whose custom had been to mutilate his prisoners, Israel treated him as he had treated others, and so was it with Israel himself. Ahab and Jezebel, who slew the prophets, perished ignominiously, and their blood was licked by dogs. Before Christ's coming, and afterwards, Israel experienced what he did to others.

"Israel destroyed the temple of the body of their best and greatest Friend, an awful miracle which sin wrought, and their temple of stone and gold was rased to the ground. On the hill of Golgotha they shed blood, and the Mount Moriah,

---

[1] The late Prof. Paulus Cassel, of Berlin. His erudition, versatility, and genuine disinterested love for his nation have been acknowledged by the Jews themselves.

which their fathers' holy footsteps had trodden, became a desolation. As they had shed blood, so were they for centuries slain like sheep of the slaughter, both in the East and in the West, both by Christians and Mohammedans. The prophecy of Moses in Deut. xxviii. 66 was fulfilled in a hundred places: 'Thou shalt fear day and night, and shalt have none assurance of thy life.' A Jewish author in Spain makes a Christian servant say that he had been told by his masters that since Jews had put the Saviour to death it was no crime to murder a Jew.

"They struck the Innocent One, and fearfully has the rod of retribution been laid on their own backs. A Jewish poet of the Middle Ages mourns:

> "'We are beaten with rods,
> The wounds bleed.'

Even Queen Christina of Sweden allowed her attendants wantonly to beat her Jewish physician as if he were a fox. In Frankfort in the eighteenth century Spencer strongly reprobated from the pulpit the system of beating and mocking Jews, so that they could not pass through the streets without insult. Fools full of iniquity had struck the Lord in the face, and how has this been visited upon them! In the Middle Ages it was customary at Toulouse to give a Jew a violent blow on the face in the name of the community, so much so that death often ensued; and this was specially done at the seasons of Christmas, Good Friday, and the Feast of Assumption.

THE BADGE OF SHAME 87

"They demanded the liberation of Barabbas, and they, who in their paschal hymns so beautifully styled themselves the sons of freedom, became the general slaves of the empire. They made Christ bear His cross on His weary way, and, for a long, long time, whilst longing and waiting from morning to evening, and from evening till morning, have they borne the ignominious cross as a mark on their hats and on their garments.

"In the Middle Ages they were forced in some countries to have the letter T on their clothes to distinguish them. It served as a memorial to represent the truncated cross, and had reference to the words of the prophet Ezekiel: 'Go ye through the streets of Jerusalem, and set a mark upon their foreheads.' It is asserted that in the East they have been branded in the face and neck like horses, which, however, has been also done to Christians by Moslem princes. Hokem Biamsilla compelled them to wear the image of the golden calf on their breasts.

"It was the most degrading punishment when Israel elevated Christ on the cross—the most exalted of their high priests; and from that moment how degraded has Israel been, for he degraded himself when he defiled his Priest and Prophet! Jews in the Middle Ages were considered unworthy of being hanged on the same gallows with Christians. In Wiesthümer they were ranked with vile women and hangmen. In a Bavarian tax register of 1458 they are classed under 'things for sale' between trout and veal! Were not they the people who murmured against Jesus because He ate with publicans and sinners? and for 1,500 years they had to pay a poll tax, and form an important article in the revenue of the State.

"This tax was only removed in 1813 in Saxony, and originated in the principle of the Swabian law that the Emperor, like every sovereign prince before him, was the successor of the Emperor Titus, and consequently the master of their life and death, and this claim they could only redeem by paying every third penny they had. In a proclamation of Albrecht Achelles of Brandenburg, it is said these words occur: 'Be it known throughout the Empire in the event of a king of the Romans being chosen—that he may either burn all the Jews according to ancient custom, or show them mercy in allowing them to purchase their lives by paying the one-third of all they possess.'

"They stoned Stephen and Paul, and in the course of time every one of these stones finds its way back upon their own heads.

"In Beziers on Palm Sunday, the custom was for Christians to have a stone-throwing at the Jews. The bishop gave his blessing to the people in these words: 'Throw stones and manfully revenge Christ's shame'; and with the blessing of their spiritual pastor, and the permission of their prince, we can imagine it would not be done by halves.

"The many complaints that when Christians were persecuted it was not for things they had done, but for the name they bore, and that the occasional misdeeds of a few were visited upon all, over which the Fathers (Justin, Tertullian, &c.)

OPPRESSED FROM ALL SIDES

mourn so much, are constantly recurring facts in the history of the Jews. ' One Israelite is surety for another ' has become a proverb. The community suffers for the crime of an individual.

"Dickens, in one of his tales, makes a pious Jew speak thus : ' In Christian countries Jews are not treated like other people, for they say, " This is a bad Greek, but there are good Greeks. Such a one is a bad Turk, but good ones can be found." When they talk of Jews it is not so. They find out the bad amongst us easily enough—in every nation is it not easy to discover the bad?—but people take the worst amongst us as specimens of the best, and accept the vilest among us to represent the noblest, and say Jews are all alike.'

"Tertullian and Origen defended the early Christians from another reproach—that of being deficient in patriotism, and not to be depended upon as citizens. This accusation has been engraved on the hearts of Jews by all parties, with sword and with pen. When the Arabs took possession of Spain, the blame was laid on them. Yet they were even killed because they did not surrender the Spanish fortresses after the flight of the Goths. In the year 1849, many of the inhabitants of Komorn were slain in the Hungarian revolution because one Jew, whose sympathies were Austrian, supported the besiegers, whilst at the same time every Jewish community was taxed by Prince Windishgrätz, where a single Jew was found who sympathised with Kossuth.

"The accusation brought against the Christians by the heathen and Jews, of drinking blood at their meetings, was a horrible misrepresentation of the Lord's Supper. Justin Martyr appealed to the Jew Trypho to bear witness that it was not true ; and how has this accusation recoiled upon the Jews, of whom thousands have lost their lives in consequence of their being supposed to drink blood, though there has never been a shadow of foundation for it.

"The Jews vilified Christ and His disciples, and gave them names of reproach ; and their own honourable name of 'Jew,' which had won such glory in the heroic time of the Maccabees, the possession of which was the Apostle's boast, and which is borne by the Lion of Judah, has become a term of opprobrium. They who bear it are sometimes themselves ashamed of it, as of a word of reproach. A French writer, wishing to describe with moral bitterness the extent to which corruption, love of money, and dishonesty prevailed in the time of Louis Philippe, entitled his book *Jews, the Kings of the Time*.

"Rothschild has been called king of the Jews, and also the Jew of the kings ;[1] but the crown of thorns which has encircled this name throughout history, with burning shame and reproach for young and old, in the schools and in life, in books and newspapers, has not yet lost its power to pierce.

"An idea prevalent in former times has latterly been revived—that Judas, who betrayed his Master,

[1] It may not be out of place here to mention the German saying referred to in the text—"The Jews used to have one king ; now the kings have one Jew."

was a type of the Jewish people in their history; but this is utterly erroneous, for Judas only typifies the treachery of those who, professing to be disciples, betray their Master, from fear of man or self-made wisdom.

" The Jewish priests and elders who gave money to set aside the Saviour who came to them, gave money to lose love, offered money to betray the True One, have imprinted the judgment that befell them on the history of the nation. Israel had soon nothing to trust in but money. Money became his breastplate, his sword, his refuge. It saved the people from death, but did not ennoble their life. For money Israel sold Him who brought the noblest freedom, and by money he purchased a tolerated servitude. Money was his protection and his bitterest enemy. He was trodden under foot if he had it not, envied and hated if possessed of it. Henry III. of England pulled out the teeth of Jews in York till they gave up all their wealth, and his successors banished them from the kingdom. They were drained of all they had, and then punished for having nothing. Usury was their exclusive privilege, and they were made to suffer for exacting it. Money is their power and their enemy.

" Such it has been, and such it is at the present time."

People have not failed to draw the conclusion that the legendary wandering Jew is a type of his nation; but the one-sidedness of this view is apparent. Israel is no aged wanderer in the world's history, *but an ever youthful prophet of the judgment and the grace of God* who appeared in his midst—like the legendary handkerchief on which remained the impress of our Lord's features ; but this handkerchief was a banner of glory and holiness. Israel's history is the impression of the scars of judgment—a history so far of the cross, but through the Christ, who has never ceased to yearn over them, and on whose cross was inscribed *Jesus Nazarenus Rex Judæorum*—a relationship which He has never renounced, and which is *indissoluble*—it shall yet become one of victory and of glory.

CHAPTER V

ISRAEL'S SUFFERINGS IN FULFILMENT OF DIVINE FORECASTS AND AN OBJECT-LESSON TO CHRISTENDOM

THERE are yet two points in connection with Israel's night of weeping which I must emphasise at the risk of repetition before proceeding to the second section of our psalm.

1. Israel's sorrows and sufferings are not only due in the first instance to God's righteous and retributive anger against His people; but are *in fulfilment* of prophetic forecasts, predictions, and warnings, some of which were uttered at the very beginning of their national history.

If it be true indeed, as their own prophets and historians pathetically complain, "that under the whole heaven hath not been done as hath been done upon Jerusalem" (Dan. ix. 12); and that "the misfortunes of all men from the beginning of the world, if they be compared with those of the Jews, are not so considerable as they were," what is this but a fulfilment of the solemn and awful words of God through Moses: "If thou wilt not observe to do all the words of this law that are within this book, that thou mayest fear *this glorious and fearful Name, Jehovah, thy God*, then Jehovah will make thy plagues wonderful, and the *plagues of thy seed, even great plagues*, and of long continuance, and sore sicknesses and of long continuance." And again in the same prophecy : " Because thou servedst not the Lord thy God with joyfulness, and with gladness of heart, by reason of the abundance of all things : therefore shalt thou serve thine enemies which the Lord shall send against thee, in hunger and in thirst, and in nakedness, and in want of all things : and He shall put a yoke of iron upon thy neck, until He have destroyed thee " (Deut. xxviii. 47, 48, 58, 59).

2. The history and experience of Israel in dispersion is intended of God to be an object-lesson and warning to Christendom. This is one reason why the Shepherd of Israel—who has had His eye on his erring flock even during the period of their banishment from His presence—has so ordered their wanderings that the great bulk of the Jewish nation has for so many centuries been found in countries in which, nominally at least, the Name of Christ has been professed.

We are thankful for the confirmation of Scripture and for the light thrown on the Word of God by recent historical and monumental discoveries ; but the most eloquent monument to the faithfulness of God and to the everlasting truth of His holy Word is the Jew : and there is an inscription more striking and legible than many which can be found written on papyrus or graven on rock—an inscription two millennia long, consisting of the history of the Jewish nation since their dispersion, written for the most part in their own blood.

And how does the inscription read? Or in other words, what is the testimony which Israel in dispersion, and during his night of weeping, bears to the Christian nations? Some of Israel's modern leaders and teachers would have us believe that the dispersion, instead of being an act of God's judgment upon the nation on account of their sin, and an expression of His displeasure, was intended to be, and had indeed proved, a means of blessing to the world, because the nations have in this manner learned to know the One true and living God. Thus even in the prayer-book of the Jewish " Reform " community in Berlin we find this remarkable passage : " Exalted high was the Light of Thy knowledge (O God) in Jerusalem, and in the midst of Israel ; but a dark and all-pervading night rested beyond his boundaries, and no ray of Thy light reached the peoples round about. But behold ! the mighty and exalted Temple building falls—the pillars which bare its domes brake in pieces—Thine hand, O God, has broken it into fragments. Lamenting, the sons of Israel go forth into the distant land ; by the waters of Babylon they sat and wept, but when they returned to the place of Thy Temple in order to build it up anew, then Thy right hand laid hold of them again, and scattered them on the face of the whole globe—even as far as the sun sends forth his rays. And behold, love sprang up where hatred was sown, and light where night had rested ; the

Sun of Righteousness rises over the earth."[1] And so, in a prayer for the Sabbath Day we read: "Thou hast called us as priests of Thy law, O Father of Mankind ! .... that we might bear witness in our endeavours and strivings."

In the same spirit many, especially of the "Reformed" Rabbis, and Jewish writers, speak boastfully of Israel's "mission" among the nations, and of the time when *through them* the Messianic era (for these Jews have given up the hope of a *personal* Messiah) shall be ushered in on the earth. But this is mere delusion; for, as I have said elsewhere, "Neither from the 'Orthodox' Talmudic Jews, who may be regarded as the successors of the Pharisees, nor yet from the progressive or 'Reform' Rabbis, who are no improvement on the Sadducees of the time of our Lord, did the Gentiles learn to know of the true and living God, but from the Jewish apostles of Jesus Christ, the *true* Light of the World, whose glory these Rabbis have done their utmost to hide and misrepresent before their people, and from such Jews whose names the nation cast out as evil, and who had to take upon them the same reproach of their Messiah, and follow Him 'outside the camp.'" It is a notorious fact also that these Rabbis and Jewish leaders who boast in having a "mission" to the nations are doing absolutely nothing to bring the knowledge of God, or to spread abroad their law, among the

---

[1] *Gebetbuch der Jüdischen Reformgemeinde zu Berlin*, pp. 38, 39. The edition from which I am translating is the *Neue Ausgabe*, Berlin, 1885, Selbstverlag der Jüdischen Reformgemeinde.

A WITNESS TO CHRISTENDOM

Gentiles ; and that since the rejection of Christ and the destruction of Jerusalem, while the Gospel of Christ has continued its triumphal march among the nations, the synagogue has been struck with impotence and unbelieving Israel with barrenness.

The day *is* assuredly coming when the people whose calling *it is* to be " a kingdom of priests and an holy nation " (Exod. xix. 6) *shall* show forth God's praise, and be the instrument in His hand to spread abroad the knowledge of God among all nations ; but the law to which they will then " bear witness " (to use the language of the Reformed Prayer-Book quoted above) will be the new law of the Spirit of Life in Christ Jesus, and the spirit in which all Israel will then go forth among the nations will be the spirit of the Apostle Paul, who said : " God forbid that I should glory, save in the cross of our Lord Jesus Christ, by whom the world is crucified unto me and I unto the world."

Till then, as already shown, Israel is a witness chiefly to God's righteous judgment, and the solemn inscription which is written over the history of the Jewish people since their dispersion for the instruction and the warning of Christendom is this : Jehovah is a righteous and faithful God —faithful in carrying out His threatenings as in fulfilling His promises ; it is an awful thing to fall into the hands of the living God when once these hands are stretched out in judgment—whether it be against a nation or an individual. " Behold, therefore, the goodness and the severity of God ; on them which fell severity ; but toward thee goodness, if thou continue in His goodness ; otherwise thou also shalt be cut off."

Would to God Christendom had read this inscription and had laid to heart this warning ! Then it would not have developed into what it is ; then it would not have fallen into the very sins and errors—in an even more intensified form—which brought about the banishment and long-continued sorrows which came upon Israel.

" Nor let the Church Christian "—says Bishop Horne, speaking of the desolation of the vineyard, (Psa. lxxx. 13)—" imagine that these things relate only to her elder sister. Greater mercies and more excellent gifts should excite in her greater thankfulness, and call forth more excellent virtues ; otherwise they will serve only to enhance her account and multiply her sorrows. If she sin and fall after the same example of unbelief, she must not think to be distinguished in her punishment, unless by the severity of it. She may expect to see the favour of Heaven withdrawn, and the secular arm, instead of supporting, employed to crush her ; her discipline may be annihilated, her unity broken, her doctrines perverted, her worship deformed, her practice corrupted, her possessions alienated, and her revenues seized, till at length the word be given from above, and some Antichristian power be unchained to execute upon her the full vengeance due to her sins."

But not *only* to God's righteous judgment does Israel in dispersion bear witness. How thankful, for instance, even true Christians should be that in these days of increasing unbelief in the supernatural, when attempts are being made even within the professing Christian Church itself to reduce all the early records of biblical history into myths and legends, that we have still a whole nation in our midst who *embody all their past history in their present*, and who, by their very existence and solemn rites and observances, bear witness in a thousand ways to the historic truth of those early Scriptures, which, in the providence of God, they have preserved for us.[1] And in these days also, when even theological professors coolly assert that it is doubtful whether Abraham was an actual personality, and when a canon of the Church of England can coolly assert that to him the actual existence and personality of Moses is "unproved and improbable," and when others who condescend to admit the existence of Moses as an historical personality confidently declare that he had very little or nothing to do with the giving of the Law—how thankful, I say, we should be that to this day there is a whole people scattered throughout the earth who whenever they name Abraham always add *Abinu*—" Abraham, our father " ; and whenever they speak of Moses say, *Moshe-Rabenu*—" Moses, our *teacher*, or *Law-giver*," as if in solemn protest against those extreme, unreasonable, and unjustifiable theories which are now being palmed off in the name of criticism !

And in this materialistic age, when men are denying God, not only as Redeemer but as the

[1] This section to the end of this chapter is transferred here from the author's small book *A Divine Forecast of Jewish History*.

Creator, it is something to have a nation who throughout their history have kept the seventh day as a reminder and testimony that in six days the Lord created the heavens and the earth, but rested on the seventh day.

How significant also are the various festivals which Israel continues to observe ! For instance, there is the Passover, which celebrates the great historical event of the Exodus and the wonders which God wrought for them in bringing them out of Egypt ; there are the Feasts of Weeks and of Tabernacles, which commemorate the experiences in the wilderness, and their entrance into the promised land ; and the many other rites and observances which could only have originated in actual facts of history, of which they are mementos.

"And as they observe the festivals so they observe the law of Moses ; and it is owing to that law of Moses that they are still in existence, for Israel is not like any of the other nations. Other nations, when they have reached, as it were, their highest point, and when they have been living in great civilisation and luxury, become effete, on account of their immorality and on account of their wickedness ; but Israel has never become effete.

"The sanctities of family life endure in Israel up to this day, owing to the law of Moses, owing to the ten commandments, owing to the ordinances which God gave to His people, and to God Himself watching over them. They are physically, as they ever were, distinguished by their longevity, dis-

THE UNDYING PEOPLE

tinguished by their tenacity and vigour of purpose, distinguished by their mental freshness, so that they are able to enter into any branch of study or into any occupation of life."[1]

"God's judgment of Israel," says another Hebrew Christian brother, "is the most terrible thing in history—yet they have been preserved to this very day through the power of that very God who punished them so terribly. Here they are, a monument of the truth of God's Word—a monument also of God's faithfulness. None of the persecutions which they have endured have availed to destroy them, neither have they broken their energy, nor subdued their indomitable will, nor crushed their power of mind; and no sooner was the great pressure which the nations—so-called Christian nations—put upon them removed than we see them prosper in every country, and take leading positions in every sphere of life—in commerce and politics as well as in literature and art, showing that the Lord God has made them to be a peculiar people, a nation to be perpetuated; and that it was He who gave them nerve to endure, in order that in the future, when His grace shall melt their hearts, they may be a mighty instrument to show forth His praise. There is still visible among scattered Israel something of blessing and influence, the effect of God's training through so many centuries. Their history since the rejection of Christ is unspeakably sad; yet we cannot help noticing that in the midst of Christless Israel some

[1] Adolph Saphir.

traces of the grandeur and beauty of their fathers' house still linger.

"Behold their zeal for God, their zeal for the Scriptures, their zeal for the Sabbath Day ; behold the sacrifices which they make in order to carry out the injunctions of the Law ! Yes, there are many features in the Jewish character which we cannot explain in any other way than this—that there is still a blessing resting on them ; that the voice of God which was heard upon Sinai has still its echo in their hearts and consciences ; and that the prayers which have been offered up on their behalf, by patriarchs, kings, prophets, and saints, are still held in remembrance before the throne of God."[1]

[1] From an address by C. A. Schönberger.

CHAPTER VI

THE PARABLE OF THE VINE: THE CONTRAST BETWEEN THE PAST AND THE PRESENT

I COME now to the third and longest section of this comprehensive psalm, in which, as stated in the Introduction, the plea for God's interposition on Israel's behalf is based on the ground of His former mercies to them.

First, we have a striking picture of the time when, under the fostering care and protection of Jehovah, Israel spread themselves abroad and flourished:

"Thou broughtest a vine out of Egypt;
  Thou didst drive out the nations, and plantedst it.
  Thou preparedst room [or "didst clear room," or "the ground"] before it,
  And it took deep root, and filled the land.
  The mountains were covered with the shadow of it,
  And by its boughs the cedars of God.
  She sent out her branches unto the sea,
  And her shoots unto the river."

The Vine (or Vineyard) as an emblem of Israel is frequently found in the Old Testament, and is adopted also by our Lord in His parables in the New Testament. To the inspired writer of this psalm it has very probably been suggested by Isaiah's prophetic song on the same theme (chap. v. 1—7), to which there are manifest allusions in this psalm, and perhaps also by Jacob's blessing on Joseph, who is described as " a fruitful bough by a fountain, whose branches run over the wall " (Gen. xlix. 22).

Looking closely into this parable, we find in these eight graphic lines a summary of God's mighty acts of power and grace, and also of judgment, which He displayed in bringing Israel out of Egypt and in planting them in the land of promise.

It is in many points a parallel scripture to the 44th Psalm, where the psalmist also seeks to encourage himself and the people in their present distress and suffering by a rehearsal of God's wonderful deeds for them in the past:

"O God, we have heard with our ears [I am translating literally] our fathers have told us,
What work [or "how wonderfully"] Thou didst in their days, in the days of old.
It was Thou—with thine own hand, Who didst drive out the nations and plantedst them [*i.e.*, Israel];
Thou didst afflict the peoples and didst spread them [*i.e.* Israel] abroad."

In both psalms all the glory of Israel's deliverance from Egypt and of the original conquest of Palestine is ascribed to Jehovah.

1. Found in the uncongenial soil of Egypt, where they had been held, so to say, rooted for

centuries, God *brought them out;* the particular verb which the sacred singer employs being used both of horticulture (Job xix. 10) and, like the word " planted " in the next line, of " breaking up and removing a nomadic encampment—the pulling out the tent pins and driving them in."

It was He Himself " with His own hand " and stretched out arm who did it ! for the more we learn of the might of Egypt at the time of the Exodus, and how contrary to all human probabilities it was that Israel could ever have escaped from under the hand of the mighty Pharaohs, the more we understand how it is that in the Old Testament the Exodus, and the wonders which accompanied it, are continually referred to as the most manifest proof of the almighty power of God in exercise on behalf of His people.

And it was a display, not only of His power, but of His *grace,* for all that the sacred historians and prophets tell us of Israel's moral and spiritual condition in Egypt, and at the time of their deliverance, testifies to the fact that they did not in themselves deserve such a Divine interposition on their behalf. But in the words of another psalm :

"He remembered His holy word [of promise]
And Abraham His servant ;
So he brought out His people with joy,
And His chosen ones with singing." (Psa. cv. 43.)

2. And it was He also who did " drive out the nations " in order " to clear the ground " and make room for this vine, which His own right hand was now bringing in to plant. " By their

own sword " they never could have conquered Palestine. All the historical and monumental discoveries go to show that the region was at that time inhabited by different nations, some of them very warlike, greater and mightier than they, whom they never could have dislodged in their own strength. What the human probabilities were in reference to Israel's gaining possession of the land were stated by the spies in their report : " The people that dwell in the land are strong, and the cities are fenced in and very great : and moreover we saw the children of Anak there "—in short— " We be not able to go up against the people, for they are stronger than we " (Num. xiii. 28—31). This was all true ; their sin and guilt lay only in the fact that they left God and His promises out of account. Caleb and Joshua put the matter in its true light ; they did not under-estimate the difficulties ; they also saw the great and fenced cities, and the giants, but they said : "*If Jehovah delight in us, then He will bring us into the land, and give it unto us.*" And that the faith and confidence in God of these two were justified, is attested by history and commemorated in these two psalms and other scriptures :

"They got not the land in possession by their sword,
 Neither did their own arm save them :
 But Thy right hand and Thine arm and the light of Thy countenance.
 Because Thou hadst a favour unto them." (Psa. xliv. 3.)

3. But in the words " Thou didst drive out the nations " and " afflict the peoples," we are re-

minded not only of God's acts of power and of grace toward Israel, but of His severity and righteous judgment toward the seven nations of Canaan.

Unbelievers sometimes cavil at Scripture because of the record it contains of the destruction of these peoples, and profess themselves even unable to believe in a God who could sanction or permit such things; while modern Christian apologetes think themselves under the necessity to compromise the character and inspiration of the sacred writers by assuring us that God *never did* command Israel to uproot and destroy those nations. The simple believer, on the other hand, remembering the marvellous longsuffering which God exercised toward these Canaanites, and how for *many centuries* He had been waiting and restraining His anger because "the iniquity of the Amorite" was not yet quite full (Gen. xv. 16), cannot only exclaim:

"Great and marvellous are Thy works, Lord God Almighty; just and true are Thy ways, Thou King of Nations. Who shall not fear Thee, O Lord, and glorify Thy Name, for Thou only art holy"—

but, without holding God responsible for any single deed or particular action on the part of Israel or their leaders and judges in their relation to these doomed nations, can even see His love and concern for humanity as a whole in His acts of judgment on these corrupt peoples.

We do not regard the skilful surgeon (to use a very imperfect illustration) as a cruel man, but rather as a benefactor, when to save the man he has to cut deep and sharp in order to remove a diseased or decaying physical member ; so neither is God unjust or unkind when nations or individuals who have become wholly and hopelessly, both morally and physically corrupt, are given over by Him to utter destruction in order to prevent the festering mass from becoming a source of moral contagion and death all around.

"Behold, therefore," my reader, in these lines of the psalm, "the goodness and the severity of God"; toward these nations whom He "drove out" and "afflicted" severity, but toward Israel goodness, so long as Israel continued in His goodness ; but when Israel in their turn began to manifest signs of moral and spiritual corruption, He spared not even His own chosen people—" the dearly beloved of His soul "—but gave over generations of them to judgment, and the whole nation to long-continued suffering, though His purpose in reference to their future still abides.

4. But to return more directly to our psalm, which goes on to dilate on the wonderful way in which this slip of a "vine," which the great Husbandman transplanted from Egypt, grew and flourished under His fostering care :

> "It took deep root and filled the land,
> The mountains were covered with the shadow of it,
> And by its boughs the cedars of God.[1]
> She sent out her branches unto the sea,
> And her shoots unto the river."

[1] I prefer this rendering to that given in the Authorised and Revised Versions, and it brings out the parallelism more clearly.

BOUNDARIES OF THE LAND

In these lines we have a poetic or allegorical reference to the boundaries of the promised land, and particularly to the limits of its possession reached in the glorious days of the Solomonic empire (1 Kings iv. 24). For the "mountains" refer to the hill country of Judea in the South, "particularly the southernmost part of the same, which at the commencement of Israel's country met the traveller like a wall"[1] and the "cedars" unto which the boughs of the vine reached out stand for Lebanon in the North—the expression "of God" (translated in the Authorised Version "goodly"), used also in Psa. xxxvi. 6 of the mountains of Palestine, being intended to impress us with their loftiness and majesty, and perhaps also with the fact of God's delight in them as an outstanding feature of Immanuel's land, and as showing forth the glory of the Creator. The (Mediterranean) "sea" always stands for the western boundary of Palestine, and the "river," which is the Euphrates, for the eastern boundary. Thus, in measure at any rate, especially during Solomon's reign, and as a foreshadowing of the time when restored and converted Israel shall enter into the full possession of the whole promised land, has God's promise to them through Moses been fulfilled: "Every place whereon the sole of your foot shall tread shall be yours, from the wilderness, and Lebanon, from the river, the river Euphrates, even unto the hinder [or western] sea shall be your border" (Deut. xi. 24).

5. Compared with the beautiful past, when

[1] Hengstenberg.

Israel dwelt under the protection and favour of God, the present appears all the more gloomy. "Why," the psalmist mournfully proceeds—

> "Why hast Thou broken down her fences,
> So that all they which pass by the way do pluck her?
> The boar out of the wood doth ravage it,
> And the wild beast of the field doth devour it."

Here again the sacred writer attributes Israel's misfortunes as being due in the first instance to the withdrawal of God from their midst. So long as He was among them, "the Almighty was their defence," and His salvation was much more to them than "walls and bulwarks" (Isa. xxvi. 1). Not all the nations combined, nor all the forces of the universe, could prevail against them as long as Jehovah Himself was the Captain of their salvation, and strove with them that strove against them. But when He hid His face and withdrew from them, then their "defences were broken down," and all that passed by began to "pluck" at them.

The "boar" and the "wild beast," which latter word is found in the original elsewhere only in Psa. l. 11, are emblematic of Gentile world-power [1]—of those nations namely who in turn tread down Jerusalem and oppress Israel—the last named, which is formed from a verb which means to "move to and fro" in restless activity, pointing

---

[1] There are many other scriptures where Gentile powers are symbolised by wild beasts and birds of prey. *Cf.* Psa. lxvi. 30; Ezek. xxix. 3; Ezek. xvii.; Dan. vii., &c.

probably to the last of the four "great beasts" in Daniel's vision, whose united course make up "the time of the Gentiles"—the one "diverse from all the beasts which went before it"—the great Roman power, which is still dragging on, and is yet to be manifested in its final development under Antichrist, and which in a special manner has "devoured and brake in pieces and stamped the residue with his feet."[1]

And that which the psalmist here describes as actually taking place is exactly what the great Husbandman *threatened* to do in the pathetic and beautiful song about the vineyard uttered by Isaiah, where we also find the answer to the question expressed in the "why" in the twelfth verse. It was because after having done all that He possibly could for this vineyard He found that it brought forth only wild grapes, that He finally says: "Go to, I will tell you what I will do to My vineyard: I will take away the hedge thereof, and it shall be eaten up, and I will break down the fence thereof, and it shall be trodden down; and I will lay it waste; it shall not be pruned nor hoed, but there shall come up briars and thorns; I will also command the clouds that they rain no rain upon it. For the vineyard of Jehovah of Hosts is the house of Israel, and the men of Judah His pleasant plant; and He looked for judgment, but behold oppression; for righteousness, but behold a cry" (Isa. v. 1—7).

[1] So the Talmud understood it.

CHAPTER VII

"TURN AGAIN, WE BESEECH THEE": ISRAEL'S HOPE FOR THE FUTURE

MOVED by the picture of Israel's present oppressed and desolate condition, the psalmist breaks forth into earnest, importunate prayer for God's interposition and deliverance:

"God of Tzebaoth, turn again, we beseech Thee,
Look down from heaven and behold, and visit this vine";

as much as to say "Only turn Thyself" to look, and Thou wilt surely be moved with compassion, and wilt visit with Thy mercy and deliverance once again this Vine. But we may regard this prayer also in a more literal and personal sense. During Israel's long night of weeping God is represented as having withdrawn Himself. "I will go," He says, to quote another prophetic scripture, "and return to My place till they acknowledge their offence and seek My face"; but "He will turn again, He will have compassion on us; He will subdue our iniquities; and Thou wilt cast all their sins into the depths of the sea." And

A PATHETIC PLEA

"His going forth is sure as the morning; and He shall come unto us as the rain, as the latter rain that watereth the earth" (Hos. v. 15; vi. 3; Micah vii. 19).

In the first line of the fifteenth verse the Authorised Version has "and the Vineyard," and the Revised Version the "Stock"; but almost all modern scholars are agreed in regarding the Hebrew word *Khano*, not as a substantive, but as the imperative of the verb *Khonan*, meaning to cover or to protect, in which sense it was understood also by the translators of the Septuagint and Vulgate versions. It certainly preserves the parallelism best:

"Look down from heaven, behold and visit this Vine,
 And protect [or "maintain"] what Thy right hand hath planted.
 And the son [not branch, as in A.V., or more lit. "upon" or "over the son"; *i.e.* "let Thy protection be over him"] whom Thou madest strong for Thyself."

Once again the present wretchedness of Israel forces itself on the psalmist's mind, and he would use it also once more as a plea with God for His interposition on their behalf:

"It [*i.e.* the vine which Thou hast brought out of Egypt; the vineyard which Thine own right hand hath planted] is burned with fire, it is cut down,
 At the rebuke of Thy countenance they perish.
 Oh, let Thy hand be upon [or "over"] the man of Thy right hand,
 Upon the son of man whom Thou madest strong for Thyself."

"The Son," "the Man of Thy right hand," "the Son of Man"—primarily all these names apply to and are used of Israel. (*a*) "Israel is My son, My firstborn," was God's word to Pharaoh (Exod. iv. 22), and in Hos. xi. 1 we read, "When Israel was a child I loved him, and called My son out of Egypt." (*b*) And Israel was called to occupy the position of honour and power as the "man of God's right hand"—the true Benjamin, to which name there is a manifest allusion, and of whom it is said :

"The beloved of Jehovah shall dwell in safety by Him ;
And [Jehovah] shall cover him all the day long,
And he shall dwell between His shoulders." (Deut. xxxiii. 12.)

(*c*) And he also is the Ben-Adam—"the Son of Man" who, though "belonging to a humanity that is feeble in itself, and thoroughly conditional and dependent,"[1] is by God's power made strong for and by Himself.

But though Israel was called to be all that, they have never yet responded to their high calling ; and actually, and in their truest and deepest sense, these titles belong to the antitypical Israel—to Him who is the crown and glory of Israel, and through whom alone Israel will at last enter into the condition and experience of sonship. He is "the Son"—the only begotten of the Father, and the true and anti-typical Benjamin. Once He was the *Ben-oni*, "the Son of My Sorrow," "a Man

[1] Delitzsch.

of sorrows and acquainted with grief," but now is *Ben-jamin*, the "Man of God's right hand," exalted there in power to be a "Prince and a Saviour, to give repentance unto Israel and the forgiveness of sins." And He is also "the Son of Man," which as applied to Him has a sense and significance quite its own—the Man *par excellence*, the ideal and representative of the race.

Hence the Jewish Targum is quite right when it paraphrases the second line of the seventeenth verse in the words:

> "And upon *King Messiah*, whom Thou hast established for Thyself."

The blessed effects of God's interposition and of Israel's final outward and inward deliverance is expressed in the eighteenth verse:

> "So shall we not go back from Thee;
> Quicken Thou us, and we will call upon Thy Name."

A nation so purified in the fires of God's judgments, and which shall have passed through such a repentance and contrition of soul as are described, a nation which has tasted so deeply of the bitterness of sin, and the sweetness of the infinite love of God, which is stronger than death, as converted Israel shall have done—will take good heed never to depart from God any more, but shall continue to "follow on to know the Lord."

And this vow of future fidelity on Israel's part is confirmed by God's own sure word of promise, which says:

"TURN AGAIN, WE BESEECH THEE"

"They shall be My people, and I will be their God; and I will give them one heart and one way, that *they may fear Me for ever* for the good of them and of their children after them; and I will make an everlasting covenant with them that I will not turn away from them to do them good; and *I will put My fear in their hearts that they shall not depart from Me.* Yea, I will rejoice over them to do them good, and I will plant them in this land assuredly with My whole heart and with My whole soul." (Jer. xxxii. 38-41.)

Then also—when the spirit of grace and of supplication is poured upon them—shall Israel not only be "quickened" and "live before Him" again as a nation (Hos. vi. 2), but they shall "*call upon His Name*," or, more literally, "then will we call with Thy Name"—*i.e.*, "make it the medium and matter of solemn proclamation," as Delitzsch properly explains—the idiom being exactly the same as used of Abraham, who, wherever he went, built an altar and "called upon" (or "proclaimed aloud") the Name of Jehovah.

Yes, in that day they shall say:

"Give thanks unto Jehovah; call upon [or "proclaim"] His Name, declare His doings among the peoples, make mention that His Name is exalted.
"Oh, praise Jehovah, all ye nations;
Laud Him, all ye peoples.
For His grace [or lovingkindness] has prevailed over us;
And the truth [or faithfulness] of Jehovah endureth for ever." (Isa. xii. 4; Psa. cxvii.)

And the nations who hear them will respond:

"Hallelujah: from the rising of the sun unto the going down of the same, Jehovah's Name is to be praised."

CHAPTER VIII

THE REFRAIN

I NOW come to the refrain, which gathers up in itself the whole theme, and contains the fundamental prayer of the psalm.

It is thrice repeated, with significant variations, which mark not only the increasing intensity and fervour in the petition, but the growing faith and rising hope in the God who has promised the very things for which the psalmist here prays.

It is for that reason that many of the inspired prayers in the Psalms must also be regarded as prophecies; for they are the echo of the very words of God, and of what He actually promised that He would do.

It is because Jehovah hath revealed His purpose and "promised this goodness" unto His servants (2 Sam. vii. 27—29) that Israel's prophets and psalmists, in their intercessions for the people, "find it in their hearts to pray" such prayers unto Him.

Note the variations:

"Elohim, turn us again [or "restore us"],
And cause Thy face to shine, and we shall be saved" (ver. 3).

"Elohim Tzebaoth [God of Hosts], turn us again,
And cause Thy face to shine, and we shall be saved" (ver. 7).

"Jehovah, Elohim Tzebaoth, turn us again,
And cause Thy face to shine, and we shall be saved" (ver. 19).

Some of our hypercritical friends have somewhat stumbled at this "accumulation" and "heaping up" of the Divine names in this psalm, and are quite sure that the "addition" or "expansion" of the name Jehovah in this "Elohistic" psalm, is the touch, not of the original writer, but of a "redactor," and is proof positive that this scripture belongs to a late date. One cannot but marvel sometimes at the skill and ingenuity of some of these friends in turning order into confusion and light into darkness. Oh, there is design and fulness of meaning and beauty in this "heaping up" of God's names; for it is in these very names that the sacred writers find the basis and encouragement for all their hopes and expectations in reference to Israel's present and future: and the name of "Jehovah" in particular is their strong tower, "into which they run" and take refuge in all times of doubt and perplexity.

Now note the significance of the gradation:

1. "Elohim"—Thou fearful *almighty* God, Creator and Upholder of all things—"turn us again, cause Thy face to shine, and we shall be saved."

2. "Elohim Tzebaoth"—Thou almighty *God of Hosts*, whose chariots are "twenty thousand," even myriads of angels; who hast all the hosts of heaven, and all the forces of nature at Thy com-

mand, ready to carry out Thy behests—" turn us again, cause Thy face to shine, and we shall be saved."

3. "Jehovah Elohim Tzebaoth"—Thou everlasting, self-existing, *unchangeable* God, who hast revealed Thyself, not only in Thy might, but in Thy grace in the history of redemption; who hast entered into covenants, and given us promises to which Thou wilt ever abide faithful, though we be unfaithful and unworthy—" turn us again, cause Thy face to shine, and we shall be saved."

The prayer itself contains a twofold petition. The first is expressed in the word *hashivenu*, rendered in the Authorised and Revised Versions "turn us again"; but this verb in the Hiphil conjugation is most generally used of *a bringing back from captivity*. The prayer, therefore, which is expressed in this word is "Oh, restore us again—bring us back from our long exile and captivity—renew our days as of old, when we dwelt in safety and prosperity under Thy shepherd care."

And the answer to this fervent petition is to be found in many precious and direct promises of God, which abound in the prophetic Scriptures, and which are, so to say, echoed in this very petition. Thus, for instance, we read in Jer. xvi. 14, 15:

"Therefore, behold, the days come, saith Jehovah, that it shall no more be said, As Jehovah liveth that brought the children of Israel out of the land of Egypt: but, As Jehovah liveth that brought up the children of Israel from the land of the north, and from all the countries whither He had driven them; and I **will bring them again into their land that I gave to their fathers.**"

And, again, in Jer. xxx. 3 (to turn to no other prophetic book) God says to the prophet:

> "Write thee all the words that I have spoken unto thee in a book. For lo, the days come, saith Jehovah, that I will turn again the captivity of My people Israel and Judah, saith Jehovah ; and I will cause them to return to the land that I gave to their fathers, and they shall possess it"

—in both of which scriptures the expressions, "I will bring them again" and "I will cause them to return" are the translations of the same verb (though in another tense) as is used in the petition thrice repeated in our psalm.

We, therefore, who believe in God's Word have the sure and certain hope that the promise will be fulfilled and the prophetic prayer answered. And in this respect, as in so many others, we are different from those who make no account of God, and even from Christians who pay no heed to the sure word of prophecy.

In the elaborate work on the Jews to which I have referred more than once in these pages,[1] the writer, in summing up the present position and future prospects of the Jews among the nations, says, on the very last page :

"It would be idle to deny that, viewed as a whole, the Jewish question at the present moment stands pretty much where it has been at any time during the last eighteen hundred years. . . . If the past and the present are any guides regarding the future, it is safe to predict that for many

[1] *Israel in Europe*, by G. F. Abbott.

centuries to come the world will continue to witness the unique and mournful spectacle of a great people roaming to and fro on the highways of the earth in search of a home."

And the same spirit of pessimism in relation to their future is expressed by many Jewish writers and poets themselves. But there is no need for Israel to " roam about to and fro on the highways of the earth in search of a home." There is a home waiting for them ; but before they can return to it under the blessing of God, and enjoy rest and peace after their long wanderings, the national prodigal must first be reconciled to his heavenly Father, and confess the great sin which has been the cause of all his sorrows and sufferings.

But this brings me to the second petition in the fundamental prayer of the psalmist. The restoration of Israel to their own land, after the many centuries of dispersion and wanderings, will be a great mercy, and a wonderful event in the world's history ; but a still greater mercy and a still more wonderful thing will be their restoration to the favour of God : and this is expressed in the prayer, " Cause Thy face to shine," which is an echo and inspired reminder to God of the benediction which He Himself put into the mouth of the priests wherewith they should " bless the children of Israel," viz. :

" Jehovah bless thee and keep thee :
  Jehovah make His face to shine upon thee, and be gracious unto thee;
  Jehovah lift up His countenance upon thee, and give thee peace";

which prayer and prophecy will in the fullest and literal sense be also fulfilled in the appearing of Him who in the Old Testament is called the *Mal'ak Panav*—the "Angel of His Face" because it is the only face of God which man has ever seen, or can behold; and who, in the New Testament, is revealed as the very image of the invisible God —"the effulgence of His glory, and the express image of His substance."

"Cause Thy face to shine, and we shall be saved."

"In the light of the King's countenance is life, and His favour is as a cloud of the latter rain" (Prov. xvi. 15).

At the rising of the Sun of Righteousness all clouds and darkness must vanish. All the evils which have befallen Israel during their night of weeping have been consequent, as we have seen, on the hiding of God's face from them. "In overflowing wrath," He says, "I hid My face from thee for a moment"—one of God's moments measured by the line of eternity; but that glorious face shall yet again be turned upon them: "With everlasting kindness will I have mercy upon thee, saith Jehovah, thy Redeemer." Then we "shall be saved." Oh, yes, to behold that countenance, once marred for us more than that of any man, to walk in its light, to gaze upon it until we are transformed into the same image— that is full and perfect salvation. It is our blessed privilege now to gaze upon it by faith: "Whom having not seen we love; on whom though now

THE DAY OF UNVEILING

we see Him not, yet believing, we rejoice with joy unspeakable and full of glory ; receiving [already by anticipation] the end of our faith, even the salvation of our souls " (1 Pet. i. 8, 9). But this period of invisibility and of silence will not last for ever. The day of unveiling and of manifestation is drawing nigh, when His blessed "feet shall stand in that day upon the Mount of Olives, which is before Jerusalem on the east " ; when Israel shall behold Him with their eyes, and pointing to Him, as it were, with their hands, shall say :

"Lo, this is our God ; we have waited for Him, and He will save us : this is Jehovah ; we have waited for Him, we will be glad and rejoice in His salvation." (Isa. xxv. 9.)

And we too, my dear reader, shall see with our own eyes " the King in His beauty," and experience the very fulness and completeness of His " salvation," which shall include also the redemption of our bodies. Already we are the sons of God, but it is not made manifest what we shall be. We know, however, that "when He shall be made manifest, we shall be like Him, for we shall see Him as He is."

And "every one that hath this hope set on Him purifieth himself, even as He is pure."

APPENDICES

I

WERE THE JEWS JUSTIFIED IN REJECTING JESUS OF NAZARETH?

IN the elaborate work of over 500 pages ("Israel in Europe," by G. F. Abbott) to which I have made several references in this book and which at the time of its publication (1907) attracted a good deal of attention, the writer, a professing Christian, says (p. 43):—

"The Founder of Christianity, Himself a Jew, had appeared to His own people as the Messiah whom they eagerly expected, and with all the Divine prophecies concerning whose advent they were thoroughly familiar. They investigated His credentials, and, as a nation, they were not satisfied that He was what His followers claimed Him to be. Instead of remembering that His Jewish fellow-countrymen were, after all, the most competent to form a judgment of their new Teacher, as they had done in the case of other inspired Rabbis and prophets, the Christians proceeded to insult and outrage them for having come to the conclusion that He failed to fulfil the conditions required by their Scriptures."

I am far from condoning the insults and outrages which have been heaped upon the Jews by professing Christians, and more especially when it was done in the name of Christianity; on the contrary, I am ashamed of them and abhor them from the depths of my soul. Yet I cannot but protest against such shallow and misleading statements as the above, which only show how unfit those are to write on Jewish history who are not acquainted with the sad and tragic *religious* development of this peculiar people.

1. Alas! owing to Israel's previous alienation from God and the spirit of the prophets, as I have shown above, and the long-continued process of self-hardening through which they had passed before His advent, the majority of the nation were far from being competent to form a right judgment of their new Teacher.

2. This is shown by their very attitude and dealings with the "other inspired Rabbis and prophets." If the writer had only studied Jewish history a little deeper, he would have found that it has always been the misfortune of the Jewish nation, not only to follow false prophets, and "Rabbis" who were far from being "inspired" by the Spirit of God, but to reject and to persecute even unto death God's true prophets and messengers. On the very last page of the Jewish Scriptures (2 Chronicles being the last book of the Hebrew Bible) the sacred historian in summing up the chief causes of the calamities which ended in the destruction of the first Temple, says:

"Moreover all the chiefs of the priests, and the people, trespassed very greatly after all the abominations of the heathen; and they polluted the house of the Lord which He had hallowed in Jerusalem. And the Lord, the God of their fathers, sent to them by His messengers, rising up early and sending; because He had compassion on his people, and on His dwelling-place: but they mocked the messengers of God, and despised His words, and scoffed at His prophets, until the wrath of the Lord arose against His people, till there was no remedy."

Did they not say of Jeremiah, "This man is worthy to die," and actually seek again and again to compass his destruction because, as they said, "This man seeketh not the welfare of this people but the hurt"? (Jer. xxvi. 11; xxxviii. 4.) Did they not say to Isaiah, "See not; prophesy not. . . . get thee out of the way; turn aside out of the path; cause the Holy One of Israel to cease from before us"? (Isa. xxx. 8–11.) Is it any wonder therefore that they should have treated the greatest and the holiest of all the prophets in the same way? Of course, the Jews afterwards changed their minds and repented of their attitude to the true prophets, and so also will they yet most assuredly do of their attitude and conduct in relation to Christ.

3. It was not because Christ "failed to fulfil the conditions

required by their Scriptures" that the majority of the Jewish nation, led by their blind leaders, rejected Christ; but because of their perversion of and alienation from the spirit of this scripture (as is borne witness to by the whole Talmudic system to which He went counter) and because He failed to correspond with their own invented carnal and fantastic ideas about the Messianic kingdom which have no real basis in the Hebrew Scriptures. If they had but "searched the Scriptures" as Christ wanted them to do (John v. 39, 46, 47) with a view honestly to "investigate His credentials" in their light, they would most certainly have come to the conclusion that "they testify of Him."

4. The rejection of Christ by the majority of the Jewish nation—the sad and terrible consequence of centuries of progress in apostasy and self-hardening, for which they alone were responsible—was foreknown of God, and clearly and even minutely foretold in the Hebrew Scriptures centuries before His advent. Moreover it was the occasion of the fulfilment of the purpose of God in providing a perfect atonement, not only for Israel, but for men of all nations. The fact, therefore, of Israel's rejection of Jesus of Nazareth, instead of being an argument against His Messiahship, must, under the peculiar circumstances, be regarded as an additional proof that He is indeed the one of whom "Moses in the law and the prophets did write."

5. Lastly, let it be remembered that not *all* Israel rejected Christ. It is, alas! true that when "He came to His own"—where He had every right to expect a welcome—"they that were His received Him not"; but the "as many as received Him," to whom He gave the right and power to "become sons of God" (John i. 12), were also in the first instance men of Israel; and it was through Jewish evangelists and disciples who had all sorts of "insults and outrages heaped upon them" by the majority of their people, and most of whom had to seal their testimony with their blood, that the faith of Christ became known among the Gentiles. Now, considering that hitherto throughout the past of their history the majority of the nation has always been in a condition of apostasy from God, and that it was only through a small remnant of Israel that the purposes of God in and through

that people were carried on: we have every right to regard the minority, who did receive and follow Christ—the little "remnant according to the election of grace" as the apostle Paul calls them—*as the true Israel*, the link between the faithful in Israel in the past and the "all Israel" which after the great national repentance and conversion, when they shall look upon Him whom they have pierced and mourn, "shall be saved."

II

HEBREW CHRISTIAN TESTIMONY TO ISRAEL

Under the Direction of
DAVID BARON AND C. A. SCHÖNBERGER.

Trustees.

EDMUND BOAKE, Esq.	REV. JAMES STEPHENS.
THEODORE HOWARD, Esq.	C. A. SCHÖNBERGER.
JAMES E. MATHIESON, Esq.	DAVID BARON.

Advisory Council.

ARTHUR BOAKE, Esq.	GEORGE LINE, Esq.
ALFRED CHAPMAN, Esq.	JAMES E. MATHIESON, Esq.
GEORGE GOODMAN, Esq.	C. LEITE ROZAS, Esq.

REV. JAMES STEPHENS.

Referees.

REV. JAMES ELDER CUMMING, D.D. (St. Andrew's); CAPTAIN W. H. DAWSON (Tunbridge Wells); PREBENDARY H. E. FOX, M.A. (C.M.S.); GENERAL HALLIDAY (Blackheath); REV. D. M. McINTYRE (Glasgow); W. M. OATTS, Esq. (Glasgow); HIND SMITH, Esq.; G. F. TRENCH, Esq., B.A. (Ardfert).

This Mission to Israel, which was founded in 1893, is under the direction of David Baron and C. A. Schönberger (brother-in-law to the late Dr. Adolph Saphir), both of whom have been engaged for many years in the work of preaching the Gospel, in different parts of the world, to the people still "beloved for the fathers' sake." They are assisted by a small band of able and experienced Hebrew Christian brethren, who give proof that they are called of God to this peculiar work.

ITS AIM AND OBJECTS

are as the Lord shall enable, and supply the means, to bear witness for Christ to the Jewish people in all the lands of their dispersion, in order, by the preaching of the Gospel, to call out the "remnant according to the election of grace," and to prepare the nation for the time when "the Redeemer shall come out of Zion," and "all Israel shall be saved." To quote from an article by Mr. Schönberger : " Our mission was not intended to gain adherents to this or that particular Church, but to witness to Jews and Gentiles that *Christ is still to be Israel's King, and Israel is still to be Christ's 'own.'* We believe it, feel it, and are certain of it, and we say that the Jewish people must be evangelised by men who are in harmony with the teaching of Christ and His apostles regarding Israel, and who personally recognise that Christ, in virtue of His human descent, is the crown and glory of His people Israel." Not that there is a different Gospel for the Jews, or any other way of salvation than by repentance, grace, and faith, but that the Jewish nationality cannot be effaced, and that the Jews coming to Christ do not become 'proselytes,' but re-enter their own spiritual inheritance. The Mother-Church of all the Churches was the truly Apostolic Hebrew-Christian Church of Jerusalem, and when Israel *as a nation* shall see Him whom they have pierced, there shall be not only a renewal, but a consummation of the work once begun in the midst of this nation, and at Jerusalem.

What we continually press upon the Jews is that we believe in Christ, the Son of Man and Son of God, *not in spite of, but because we are Jews*, that Jesus is the Divine King of our people, the sum and substance of our Scriptures, the fulfiller of our law and our prophets, the embodiment of all the promises of our covenant-God. Jesus-Jehovah, Jehovah-Jesus, Jehovah-Tzidkenu, is the continual burden of our message to Israel.

"Our 'Testimony' is that *of Jews to Jews.*

"Having before our mind their singular prejudices, their peculiar ignorance regarding the Gospel of Christ, and knowing so well their traditional offence at the Cross, we try to follow the

Apostle Paul, who became a Jew to the Jews in order to win them for Christ."

Its Headquarters

are in London. Here in our large Mission House (189, *Whitechapel Road*), situated in a most prominent position on what might be called the East End promenade, a variety of efforts for Jewish men, women, and children are carried on day by day.

We may particularly mention our Bible Class, which has been carried on from seven to eight every evening for the past sixteen years (with the exception of Saturdays and Sundays, when the meetings are of a somewhat different character), and at which regular and continuous teaching in the Word of God is given. At this class, at which in the autumn and winter months as many as fifty and more Jews may be seen gathered around the Scriptures every evening, whole books of the Bible, both Old and New Testament, have been systematically gone through. Many families are also visited in their homes, and hundreds are spoken with in the streets. At intervals we visit other towns in the United Kingdom where Jews are to be found, but our hearts are chiefly set on the masses of "the Scattered Nation" in Central and Eastern Europe, and other countries, and missionary journeys are continually being made abroad. Mr. Baron, whose journals appear in *The Scattered Nation*, has himself made twenty tours in many parts of the world, always accompanied by one or two earnest, experienced Hebrew Christian brethren.

In the course of these journeys many thousands of Jews have had the Gospel of their Messiah preached to them, and many thousands of New Testaments and suitable tracts and pamphlets, such as the writings of Rabbi Lichtenstein, which are published by this Mission, circulated amongst them.

In order to supply a suitable Hebrew Christian literature for Jews we have ourselves printed and published about thirty-five very valuable books, pamphlets, and tracts in Hebrew, Yiddish, German, Hungarian, English, and French—mostly written by our own missionary brethren, and circulated very extensively in all parts of the world.

By means of our Postal Mission many thousands of the "better class" Jews in this country and in almost all other lands of the dispersion—who might never meet a missionary—have had the claims of Christ brought before them through the printed page.

The two other centres where missionaries are permanently stationed are Berlin and Budapest.

Its Character

is thoroughly unsectarian; and although we have our own views as to the necessary qualifications and proper methods for the Jewish Mission, we wish Godspeed to all who *in sincerity and truth* seek to make Christ known to the Scattered People. All who are loyal to the Bible as the Word of God; all who, in these days of failure and declension, cling to the grand old Protestant evangelical doctrines; all who out of a pure heart and in sincerity call Jesus Lord, and seek to do the will of our Father in heaven, are our brothers and sisters. We know of only one Church—"the general assembly of the first-born ones enrolled in the heavens"; and in the great work of evangelising Israel in these "latter days" we wish to co-operate with all who abide by the foundation truths of our most holy faith.

A Testimony to God's Faithfulness.

The needs of the Mission are met entirely by the *spontaneous and freewill offerings* of the Lord's people. All worldly means for raising funds are avoided as being unworthy of the cause of our great Master, Jesus Christ.

Since the foundation of the Hebrew Christian Testimony to Israel, not a penny has been spent in advertising for funds; we send about no deputations; we have no "Auxiliaries," "District Associations," or "Collectors" (though we do not mention these as judging or condemning others, who in their own way may also be doing the work of Christ); we have never yet appealed to anyone personally for money, and yet from year to year, as the work has grown and its needs have increased, the Lord has been mindful of His own work and His servants engaged in it, and has moved the hearts of His children in all parts of the world *spontaneously* to send their freewill offerings, in many cases accompanying their gifts with words of cheer, which have been more precious than silver and gold, because they speak of continual prayer and intercession going up for us, and the work, to the throne of God.

The way the large needs of this Mission have hitherto been met has been a continual testimony to all concerned that we have still to do with the same living, prayer-hearing God of Israel who gave His people manna in the wilderness, and water out of the rock.

An outstanding proof of this we had also in connection with the building of our new Mission House. It cost £9,000, and there has never been a penny debt upon it. For that, too, no appeals were made and the only place where any statement of the need appeared was our own quarterly, *The Scattered Nation*.

About £300 are needed *every month* for the current expenses of the work at home and abroad, and although we have no visible resources whatever to rely upon, we are confident that the Lord will still be mindful of us, and, out of His own fulness, supply our every need.

All the money contributed is spent in the actual and direct needs of the Mission, the support of the workers, and the relief of the poor.

For the sake of Jewish friends especially, into whose hand this book may fall, Mr. Baron feels it right to add that *he has not from the beginning of the "Hebrew Christian Testimony to Israel" taken a penny from the Mission for his own use. Nor does he receive a salary from any Mission or Society whatsoever.*

Contributions will be gratefully received by the Hon. Treasurer, A. BOAKE, Esq., Highstanding, Loughton, Essex; by C. A. Schönberger, 90, Mount View Road, Stroud Green, N.; or by David Baron, "Northfield," Chorley Wood, Herts.

They may also be sent to the Publishers of *The Christian* 12, Paternoster Buildings, E.C.; or to the Bankers: Parr's Bank, Limited, 77, Lombard Street, E.C., with instructions that they be put to the account of "Hebrew Christian Testimony to Israel."

www.ingramcontent.com/pod-product-compliance
Lightning Source LLC
Chambersburg PA
CBHW070919180426
43192CB00038B/1945